Maya Techniques | Hyper-Realistic Creature Creation

ACKNOWLEDGEMENTS

Cover & book design:
Ian McFadyen & Louis Fishauf

Cover Image:
Jeff Unay

Production designer:
Diane Erlich

Primary Editor:
Marc-Andre Guindon

Development and copy editor:
Erica Fivie

Technical editor:
Rob Ormond

DVD production:
Roark Andrade, Julio Lopez

Jr. Production Coordinator:
Skye Bjarnason

Project Manager:
Carla Sharkey

Product Manager, Learning Tools and Training:
Danielle Lamothe

Director, Learning Tools and Training:
Michael Stamler

A special thanks goes out to:

Carmela Bourassa, Sylvana Chan, James Christopher, Rachael Jackson, Jay Lilley, Lorraine McAlpine, Robert Lin, Lenni Rodrigues, Margaret Rowlands, Michael Stamler, Mariann Barsolo.

Primary Editor: Marc-André Guindon

Marc-André Guindon is the founder of Realities Studio (www.RealitiesStudio.com), a Montreal-based production facility. An advanced user of both Maya and MotionBuilder software, Marc-André and Realities have partnered with Alias on several projects, including The Art of Maya, Learning Maya 6 | MEL Fundamentals, and the entire Learning Maya 7 Series. Realities Studio was also the driving force behind Pipeline Technique DVDs such as *How to Integrate Quadrupeds into a Production Pipeline* and *Maya and MotionBuilder Pipeline*. Realities created the Maya Quick Reference Guides and contributed to *Creating Striking Graphics with Maya & Photoshop.*

Marc-André has established complex pipelines and developed numerous plug-ins and tools for a variety of projects in both the film and game industries. His latest projects include the integration of motion capture for both the EA Sports Arena Football game and the Outlaw Game Series (Outlaw Volleyball, Outlaw Golf 1 and 2 and Outlaw Tennis). He served as Technical Director on *XXX2: State of the Union* (Revolution Studios), *ScoobyDoo 2* (Warner Bros. Pictures) and *Dawn of the Dead* (Universal Pictures).

Marc-André is a Maya MasterClass presenter and continues to seek additional challenges for himself, Realities and his crew.

Authors Special Thanks:

Eric Miller:

Danielle Lamothe, Paul Thuriot, Jeff Unay, Andy Jones, Rudy Grossman, Joe Harkins, Eric Hanson, Nick Lloyd, Jake Rowell, Adam Sidwell, Carmela Bourassa, Julio Lopez, Roark Andrade, Skye Bjarnason, Erica Fyvie, Yojiro Nishimura, Max Simms, Tim Coleman, Jeff Bernstein, Alvaro Planchart, Alex Alvarez, Darin Grant, all of my good friends from Digital Domain, Sony Pictures Imageworks, Gnomon, and the rest of this ever expanding, super talented cg industry. And most of all, especially to you reading this, thanks for checking out this book, and I hope you got as much out of it as we tried to put into it! Thanks!

"To my amazing, brave and spirited father, Stephen Miller, a man full of character that I've always looked up to, who just unexpectedly passed away. I love you dad. To my wonderful mother for always supporting what I've stood for and teaching me to believe in my dreams, and my lovely wife Monica for being my life partner and eternal soul mate."

-Eric Miller

Paul Thuriot:

Thanks to Jeff and Erick, and all of the Alias LearningTools crew and special thanks to Tara Forth for being there for me.

Jeff Unay:

Thanks to Diana for her support and for allowing me to stay up waaaay past my bedtime to work on this stuff, to Danielle and Carmela from Alias for hookin' all this stuff up - you two have been awesome to work with, to Yojiro from Alias Japan for allowing me to see their beautiful country - twice! - and for taking me to the coolest hangout in Tokyo, the Cavern Club, to Rudy Grossman for all of those late nights at Expressaholic in Wellington to work on Alias stuff, to Paul Thuriot and Erick Miller for including me to work with them on the Hyper-Real series and to all my friends at Tippett Studio, Weta Digital and EA Canada for inspiring me every single day at work. You guys are the coooolest!

FOREWORD

Danielle Lamothe | Product Manager, Learning Tools and Training

Hyper-real is defined as something imaginary or incredible portrayed in a vividly realistic and believable manner. It is making the unreal, real. As the technology used to make movies continues to improve, so too does the audience's level of sophistication. Gone are the days when a reaction shot and some gloomy music could trigger screams of terror from the audience. That's not to say that a good reaction shot and gloomy music no longer have a purpose in *storytelling*. They do, and likely will continue to be important *components*. But at some point, if the film doesn't show us the monster, today's audience will likely walk away unsatisfied, muttering about a lack of budget for special effects.

The special features of hundreds of DVDs may indeed have educated today's viewer. Most of us know that while a *superhero* can fly, the actor portraying him cannot. Yet, *filmgoing* has always been about the suspension of disbelief. We are willing to believe anything, as long as the filmmaker doesn't break our trust. Don't show us the boom, and don't hide bad effects with bad lighting. Show us something we can believe, and we will.

In order to make us believe, today's artists have an impressive toolkit at their disposal. From sympathetic robots and talking trees, to enormous spiders and boys straight from hell, Jeff Unay, Paul Thuriot, and Erick Miller have helped create some of film's greatest illusions. And, like so many of today's top modelers, animators, technical directors and programmers, they've chosen Maya as their tool. They've also shown an *incredibly generous* willingness to share their production secrets with *you*, their peers and aspiring artists. This book is the fruit of a project that started out as a 90-minute presentation at Siggraph in 2004. Erick Miller and Paul Thuriot had presented a class the year before and, forgetting the workload of presenting, decided they'd do it again. Erick was going to do a class on realistic facial animation. He then enlisted Jeff Unay to create a model he could use and Paul Thuriot came back to build the body rig. They established a pipeline, collaborating together across oceans and continents via phone and email, and built a very frightening beast, indeed.

This book brings the Hyper-Realistic Series to you in one convenient volume. Gain insight into the techniques chosen by today's top artists. From the step-by-step instructions to the video clips of the artists at work, you'll see their workflows and get tips firsthand. You'll also get to work with the MEL™ scripts they've created, opening and modifying the scene files in order to gain a deeper understanding of your options as an artist working on photo-realistic projects. *I hope you are inspired enough to create the fantastic character that may punctuate your dreams.* See you at the movies!

Danielle Lamothe
Product Manager, Learning Tools and Training

AUTHOR

Erick Miller | Character Setup Supervisor, Sony Pictures Imageworks

Erick Miller, Character Setup Supervisor at Sony Pictures Imageworks, has been a Maya® user since its inception at version 1.0. Currently, Erick is finishing the all-CG Sony Pictures® Animation feature, *Surf's Up*. Prior to *Surf's Up*, while at Imageworks, Erick did facial rigging for the all-CG feature, Monster House, and also built a muscle and skin system for the visual effects feature *Ghost Rider*® . The muscle and skin system is currently being used in other upcoming feature films, including the all-CG medieval fantasy/adventure epic, *Beowulf*, directed by the acclaimed Academy Award-winning director, Robert Zemeckis. Before Sony Pictures Imageworks® , Miller worked at Digital Domain® where he contributed to several groundbreaking effects projects including a crowd animation and rendering system, and a plug-in pose space deformation system. He created the Maya crowd pipeline for *The Day After Tomorrow* and muscle based facial rigging for a photo-realistic Michael Jordan Superbowl commercial. He was also the Lead Character TD for a series of Disney 50th anniversary commercials, and with his team, created a full squash and stretch 3D cartoon character rigging pipeline. As a Lead Character TD for the feature film, *I, Robot*, Erick was responsible for the hero facial rigging of the fully CG, photo-realistic main character, "Sonny", in addition to much of the character based Maya pipeline, including the crowd system, and many scripts, plug-ins, and character based tools.

I Robot proved to be a professional highlight for Miller. "I was on the show from beginning to end and there were a lot of challenges, like the photoreal facial setup," he explains. "Plus, I was a lead so I had to supervise a group of people. We worked really hard – we re-designed the pipeline at Digital Domain. I got to work with some amazing people and the CG turned out well."

CG turning out well is a theme of Miller's career. Originally an art major, he started taking computer science courses and transferred to the Academy of Art College in San Francisco. As such, he understands the delicate balance between art and technology that frames all successful CG work.

"No matter how technical you are and how much you can program," he says, "if you're doing computer graphics, especially if you're doing character setup or even if you're just writing source code, you should be creative enough to really understand the artistic process behind it all. I'm from the school of thought that you should be an artist more than you should be a technician, that imagination is much more powerful than knowledge. And, that you can learn all the technical things you need to if you're motivated to learn them. But being creative is something that you really have to just know beforehand in order to achieve the results that you want."

Creatively, facial rigging poses several challenges since so much is emoted from facial expressions and the eyes. For Miller, the challenge is part of the appeal: "A character speaks from his face and the life of a character really is encapsulated in the eyes. In order to rig a photoreal face to make it realistic enough to animate a full range of emotion (as well as lip-synched dialogue), is an interesting challenge; it's also a place where a lot of times CG work falls short and we've seen that happen a lot recently. The devil's in the details as far as that stuff goes."

Remembering the details is an important component for the future of the industry. With the plethora of CG features being created on a continual basis, it's essential that the quality never be compromised. He says: "I think there will, unfortunately, be some CG features that will fail in the upcoming years, and it will affect our industry because right now everyone is making a CG feature since they think that's the key to success, the fact that it's CG, but I think most people hopefully understand the key to making a successful film is simply making a great product – that still means really good CG, but more importantly, a great, well written and well directed story."

Some of Erick's favorite duties include advanced character setup, facial rigging, and modeling complex skin deformations. Besides character setup, Erick also enjoys connecting his creative knowledge with MEL™ scripting, Maya's API, and other external programming languages and C/C++ APIs to further advance a character based pipeline. He has also successfully created and led several Alias MasterClasses at Siggraph. "It's fun," he says, "Alias is a great company. There's always something new about the software to share. It's a lot of work to do this stuff, but it's worth it because it's fun. If it helps other people in some way, then it's worth all the work."

Q & A with Erick Miller:

1. What favorite movie from childhood do you wish you could remake?
Clash Of The Titans

2. What music do you listen to when you're working?
Drum&Bass, Punk, Classical, HipHop, Alternative, Rock... you name it, as long as it's catchy, progressive, and sounds cool

3. What book would make a brilliant CG film?
The original DragonLance Chronicles trilogy could be a cool vfx film, if written, cast, and directed well, it could be really wicked.

4. Do you have any hobbies (unrelated to CG)?
Taking exotic trips around the world, hiking & playing tennis with my wife (not at the same time, although that could be fun to try, too).

5. What skill/talent do you wish you had?
Telepathy, psychokinesis, and any other cool psionic mind powers.

AUTHOR

Jeff Unay | Character Modeling Supervisor, Electronic Arts (EA)

Jeff Unay is a passionate artist and Maya enthusiast. He most recently accepted a position as Character Modeling Supervisor with Electronic Arts, Vancouver. Most recently, Jeff completed work as a Senior Modeler with Weta Digital working on Peter Jackson's remake of *King Kong*. Specializing in character/creature creation, his work can be found on film, television, and in video games. For his work in this book, the creation of the beast, he looked to his favorite artists and sculptors as well as nature for his inspiration. "We studied many different animals during the conceptualization stage of the new beast and really wanted to focus on capturing some of the intricate facial motion of the animals, mainly in the areas of the face where the skin reacts to the contracting, stretching and relaxing of the muscles. Those details in mind influenced the new look of the beast," he says. "For example, the beast now has specific wrinkles on its muzzle, and we wanted those wrinkles to move in a way that would give the illusion of an underlying muscle, fat and skull structure existing for the wrinkles to travel over. It was a lot of fun playing around with that."

For this design, he considered the resolution when assessing what it was that he wanted to achieve: "The resolution of the new design, or of any design really, is based on production needs so it's always going to vary. In our case, we wanted to create a topology that was efficient but also had a high level of complexity in the mesh, having lots of different folds and wrinkles traveling into each other," he explains. "If you want areas of your model to move in a specific way, chances are you're going to have to have a resolution that will support that need. If the resolution is too light in those areas, the complexity of the motion can only go so far."

Learning how to go further and teaching students to do the same has been a cornerstone of his career. After receiving a B.A. in Advertising and Graphic Design from Loyola University New Orleans and an A.S. in Computer Animation from Full Sail Real World Education in Orlando, Unay has taught Organic Modeling to MFA students at the Academy of Art University in San Francisco and has also presented several Alias® MasterClassTM sessions at Siggraph® and 3December® .

Currently, he's excited about new Maya 7 features like being able to paint weights on blend shapes: "Everyone claims that Alias put that in because they asked for it!" he jokes. "I think I've heard that, no kidding, at least three or four times from different people. You tell any modeler or character TD out there that Maya now has paintable blend shapes and their eyes get big and they say: 'Oh, cool!' The tool is one of many that leads to a more intuitive workflow. Sculpting transitions from one blend shape to the next is now a lot more flexible.

There are other new Maya 7 features worthy of getting excited about: transferring skin weights between two different topologies, a faster wrap deformer, and a faster Sculpt Polygon Tool. "Alias does a great job of listening to their user base and you can look at the polygon tools as a good example," Unay says. "There's a lot of new ring selection tools, split tools, all those things built into Maya. It makes things a lot easier and faster and more efficient."

He offers up some of his suggestions for successful workflows: "Creating all of the primary and secondary forms of your character on the geometry level and then achieving the finer tertiary detail in displacement maps is a production-tested technique. If you want to create fine wrinkles on the face that will move in a subtle manner, animated displacement maps can work great for this. Adding some on the forehead or outer area of the eye can add that extra bit of realism to your character."

Even though Unay has a strong grounding in both the artistic and technical facets of this work, he knows there's always room for growth and improvement. "Now I'm trying to focus all of my energy more toward the technical side of things," he says. "I've always considered myself to be an artist, but in this industry you have to have a good mixture of both. Some of the people that I've worked closely with that I admire in this industry, like Andrew Camenisch, Sven Jensen and Florian Fernandez, just to name a few, are highly skilled artists and very technical people as well."

Q & A with Jeff Unay:

1. What favorite movie from childhood do you wish you could remake?

I have so many favorite movies from childhood, like *Clash of the Titans*, *Conan the Barbarian*, *Enter the Dragon*, *The Warriors*, *Big Trouble in Little China*, but I couldn't imagine anyone redoing those films. I've always loved the movie Nightbreed from 1990 because of all the great creature designs, but the story seemed so incomplete. It'd be cool to do an insane monster-filled sequel to that.

2. What music do you listen to when you're working?

I probably listen to my favorite soundtracks while working more than anything, like *Kill Bill*, *Conan the Barbarian*, *Life Aquatic*, *The Lord of the Rings* and *Reservoir Dogs*. I've also been on a big audio books and Johnny Cash kick lately.

3. What book would make a brilliant CG film?

Hard Boiled by Frank Miller and Geof Darrow instantly comes to mind, although I could see that as a 30-45 minute short movie. Boy, that would be intense! Darrow's artwork gives you such a clear idea of how visually complex a CG movie of this comic could be. Alright, that does it...who out there wants to work on this with me?!!!

4. Do you have any hobbies (unrelated to CG)?

I'm a huge baseball freak, what can I say? I'm a die-hard Cubbies fan. I've also been playing a lot of basketball lately. We had a solid group of basketball nuts at Weta that I'll really miss playing with.

5. What skill/talent do you wish you had?

I wish I had the design sensibilities and drawing skills of some of those uber-talented concept artists out there today, like Kenneth Scott, Jordu Schell, Carlos Huante and Paul Richards, and also have the math background and programming capabilities of some of the guys I've worked with at Tippett and Weta. They all serve as great industry role models for me. I also wish I could hit a baseball 500 feet, but then again it's probably a good thing that I can't because I probably wouldn't have gotten into this industry in the first place

AUTHOR

Paul Thuriot | Associate CG Supervior, Electronic Arts (EA).

 "When I say creating the illusion of realism, what I mean is, when you're doing this stuff don't go for truly real. If you try and hit realism you'll never get it, it just won't happen. Take a couple of steps back, look at what you're doing. It's just like painting – when you try and paint naturally, it's better to just express yourself in it as well," says Paul Thuriot, Associate CG Supervisor at Electronic Arts (EA). Thuriot should know – he holds a B.A. in drawing and painting and a Masters degree in computer animation. His artistic and technical expertise has been brought to bear on several complex projects. Before joining EA, he was the Puppet/Creature Supervisor at Tippett Studio where he contributed to the award-winning blockbuster *"Carl & Ray"* commercials, *Blade 2, The League of Extraordinary Gentlemen,* and *Hellboy.*

A major distinction for Thuriot is that CG artists should be creating and not merely duplicating. "Add some life to the project outside of that photograph. It just makes it easier and adds a little of you into the work itself and, in all honesty, it makes it a lot more fun to work on," he explains.

It is this desire to create the new and the interesting that led him to work with Erick Miller and Jeff Unay on the Hyper-real series: "One of the main reasons why we decided to do it last year is Erick and I were talking about doing these classes and we came up with the idea that if we're going to do rigging we should do it on a cool model. Why don't we try to do some pipeline thing and build something out of that?" he says. "We threw some ideas around and Jeff's name came up. He was really into it and had the idea to create this beast character for the class that he's been wanting to do for awhile, something he sculpted and used as reference."

Once they envisioned how well the beast creature would work they decided to expand the series and add some courses. "We figured take it to the next level – that's what this year's series was. Advanced Blend Shapes with Jeff and Rudy, Facial Rigging II with Erick, my Body Setup II – it was great to get Andy to do the animation class and Jake and Nick doing the rendering and then Adam doing some pipeline stuff. It just started gelling everything together."

The larger fusion of artists and design is where he sees the CG industry going. "It's going to branch, it's going to do all kinds of things, but one of the things everyone sees happening is it becoming more interactive," he predicts. While film and game designers have always worked with and inspired each other, the line has become blurred. "When you start making movies and games the same thing almost, that's where it's going to really hit and everyone's going to get really excited," he enthuses. "When you start taking things from films and being able to do it in real time with games - real time that you can spin around, that you can interact with, you can talk to, whatever, that's where I see the future of this industry going."

"I'm hoping that's just on the horizon," he says.

Q & A with Paul Thuriot:

1. What favorite movie from childhood do you wish you could remake?

Honestly, I'm not sure...meaning the main film from my childhood that got me into the business (as for many others) already had a "remake" of sorts: *Star Wars*. That, of course, changed how we all viewed films and special effects. It was a pivotal and defining point for all of us really. With the special editions and edits that it's gone through, it's already had a face lift of sorts, along with the addition of the back story with episodes 1-3. Now to "fully" remake it, I think that would never do the story justice. And to that point, I'd really like to see NEW stories and not remakes of films we grew up on or books that we enjoyed. But that's a whole other thing.

2. What music do you listen to when you're working?

That one varies on my mood (and sometimes time of day). My musical likes span the spectrum from very airy new age-y kind of stuff to really underground metal stuff, and then, of course, everywhere in between. The majority of the stuff I like to listen to is not stuff you'll typically hear on the radio. I studied music for a time and played a lot of different styles, but always gravitated towards the heavier, more aggressive types of music. If you were looking for a list of stuff I've got on my cycle right now that people would "at least kind of" know: Cynic - still my all time favorite band, Mnemic, Fear Factory, Meshuggah, Celldweller, Delerium, Enya (hehe, yeah, get over it), Soilwork, In Flames, Al DiMeola, Lacuna Coil, Vio-lence, and Killswitch Engage. I could list tons of more "underground" stuff as well, but that could take forever trying to explain it! But basically anything that has a good groove or emotional movement of sorts works for me.

3. What book would make a brilliant CG film?

Anything with cool creatures and big battles and...well...I'm sure you get the idea.

4. Do you have any hobbies (unrelated to CG)?

There's something other than CG?! Heh...my life revolves around it (and my wife will sarcastically attest to that). From film/video games/programming/gadgets. Well, I'm into music...play numerous instruments, but mainly guitar (only have four right now–though one is a prototype for a small guitar company in California that is even named after me!) I do lots of recording, too.

5. What skill/talent do you wish you had?

If I had to sit and think about it, I guess I wish I was more "handy" with construction-type work. Like building/fixing stuff around the house. I do alright when it comes down to it...but I go out and "study" how to do it and plan, plan, plan...then do it, and the whole time I'm thinking about how much better someone who did that project for a living could do it!

Project One *Modeling*

Project Two *Rigging*

Project Three *Facial*

ABOUT THIS BOOK

Thank you for choosing Maya Techniques | Hyper-Realistic Creature Creation. This book is intended to provide the intermediate 3D software user with an inside look into professional techniques and workflows for modeling, and rigging a photo-realistic character quickly and effectively.

This book moves at a fast pace, and is designed to help you, the intermediate user, improve your understanding of high-end production techniques for modeling and rigging, and to help you understand how they relate to one another in a production pipeline. If this is your first experience with 3D software, we suggest that you begin with the Learning Maya 7 | Foundation, as a prerequisite before proceeding through the lessons in this book. If you are already familiar with Maya you can dive in and complete the lessons as written. Many of the lessons also include helpful video footage, which you will find on this book's accompanying DVD.

Updates to this book

In an effort to ensure your continued success through the lessons in this book, please visit our web site for the latest updates available: www.alias.com/learningtools_updates/

Alias Packaging

This book is based on working in Maya, However, the techniques explored here are sound regardless of your software of choice. In order to use this book, you should have one of the following software applications:

- Maya Complete 7
- Maya Unlimited 7
- Maya Personal Learning Edition 7

DVD-ROM

The DVD-ROM at the back of this book contains several resources to accelerate your learning experience including:

- MEL Scripts
- Complimentary video clips
- Support files
- Artist Interviews

Installing support files – before beginning the lessons in this book, you will need to install the lesson support files. Copy the project directories found in the support_files folder on the accompanying DVD-ROM onto your computer.

Modeling
Project One

In Project One, you are going to model a werewolf style beast as a full polygonal character.

This project will demonstrate effective, flexible and efficient techniques for creating hyper-real organic models. With an emphasis on polygonal modeling, this project will explore the modeling process from the concept stage through to pipeline integration. You will learn strategies for creating creatures and characters with an emphasis on anatomy and realism. This project will cover effective techniques and workflows for creating models that can then be easily manipulated and animated.

Once the model is finalized, the next project will explain how to create a proper control rig for the character.

Lesson 01 *Preparation and theory*

Prior to modeling in 3D, it is important to understand the various concepts involved in your project. First, you should have a good idea of what you want to do and where you want to go. It is not generally recommended to dive directly into Maya software and work by trial and error until you reach a decent result.

In this lesson you will learn the following:

- Defining hyper-real;

- What should be done in the concept phase;

- Modeling theories and key concepts;

It is important to understand why certain anatomically-based methods are needed or used in this book, rather than using non-anatomy based approaches, which could lead to less dynamically realistic and potentially more *canned* or *cartoon* results in the final product.

Here is a definition for **hyper-real**:

Above or beyond the quality of convincing existence, to the point of fantastic disbelief.

Something imaginary or incredible portrayed in a vividly realistic and believable manner.

From concept to modeling

Cartoon ● ● ● ● ● ● ● ●   **Hyper-Real**   ● ● ● ● ● ● ● ● **Photo-Realistic**

To be clear, hyper-real is believable, depending on the quality and design goals of the final model, animation and rendering style, but is not photo-realistic.

Photo-realism is easily believable to the viewer since the subject is known to already exist and have real-life references. In order for hyper-realism to be fully achieved, the rendered subject should most likely have a realistic quality of naturalism and a high potential for actual existence in real life. You should simply think of hyper-realism as *nearing or over-achieving believable photo-realism of a subject that is obviously not real*.

Concept

Before you begin to model in 3D, it is recommended to conceptualize your ideas on paper first. Some artists prefer creating character sheets that clearly define the creature's characteristics, while others would rather dive into the designing and concept stage. Either way, it is helpful to establish a few things about the creature: its purpose, personality, weight, background and history, etc.

Original sketch drawing

In addition to creating the overall design of your creature, you must also consider the media in which it will be used, technology requirements, limitations, etc. For instance, can it make use of hair, fur or cloth? All of these issues play an equally important role in its creation.

Sculpting a maquette

When you have a satisfying design on paper, you will find it helpful to sculpt a maquette of the creature using your preferred clay. This allows you to further analyze its overall structure, form and proportions well before you begin to model in 3D.

Note: *For this exercise, the beast was sculpted with Chavant NSP medium oil-based clay.*

Photographing the maquette

Now that you have a proper maquette, you should take pictures of it and then use the images as reference image planes in 3D. When taking photos, it is recommended to place your camera on a tripod that is positioned directly ahead of the maquette and then rotate the maquette at any desired angle.

Beast head sculpture

> **Tip:** You should take pictures of at least the basic 3D modeling views, such as the front, top and side views.

Once your pictures are in image editing software, you should maintain either a constant height or width for all the images, otherwise it might be confusing when used as references in Maya software. For instance, if you choose to keep their heights consistent, later in Maya, you will be able to align the images easily by setting the image plane's **Placement Fit** to **Vertical**. The camera and image plane settings will be covered more in-depth in the next lesson.

Modeling theories

Creating the perfect creature on paper or even sculpting it in clay before you sit down in front of your computer is often times unfeasible. Moreover, digital models, just like conceptual drawings and maquettes, will often go through multiple revisions. Sometimes there will be technical revisions, such as changing the topology of your model to better match the underlying muscle structure or wrinkles of the skin, or even aesthetic changes, like revising the overall structure and anatomy of the character.

The first step you will take here is to plan out the necessary edge rings for it to deform and animate as you would expect. It is a good idea to do this on paper first and then use your drawings as a guide when modeling. Or, you can take your reference photos and draw the muscle flow on top of it as shown here:

Second, you should use the maquette photographs as a starting point for your digital model. It is common to start modeling from a relaxed default pose, but in the image above the shape is quite extreme. Some believe it is easier to drop the jaw from the default pose rather than close the jaw from the open pose.

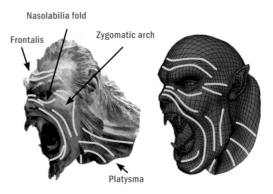

Main edge lines based on underlying muscles

The main advantage of modeling a head at its most extreme pose is that you are guaranteed that all of the necessary geometry to achieve that particular facial expression will be inserted. Then you can simply reshape it back to a relaxed closed mouth in the final model and use the extreme pose as a blend shape. If you model the closed mouth head first, you may end up modeling not enough geometry to begin with and then you are stuck with a head that is not as expressive as you first envisioned.

If you do decide to sculpt the extreme pose first for your creature, it is highly recommended that you draw out exactly what your closed mouth face will look like. If you don't do this, you may be surprised to find that your creature looks different than you had hoped. When you close the beast's mouth for the first time, it will require aesthetic adjustment to his jaw and lower face, but since you have planned for this, all you will need to do is follow the concept drawings of the closed mouth beast.

> **Note:** *When you reach this point once your character is modeled, you should not have to change its topology. If you decide to change the topology of the model, you will lose the ability to use blend shapes to bring it back to the original extreme pose.*

Key modeling concept

Before you begin with the creature's topology, there are a few key modeling concepts to keep in mind. First, you must concentrate on modeling according to muscle flow.

It is suggested to have anatomy books with you for quick referencing. Even if your model is not real, you will most likely be able to extract basic organic concepts to reproduce on your model.

When you model according to your character's muscle flow, your edge loops will help maintain the location of your muscle, which will give a more realistic look when deforming. When modeling organic characters, you should first concentrate on laying out the necessary edge loops for the muscles; once you are satisfied with the topology, you can proceed to sculpt the surface with tools like the **Soft Modification Tool** and the **Sculpt Geometry Tool**. This way, you can concentrate on the aesthetic values of the sculpture and not worry about technical issues.

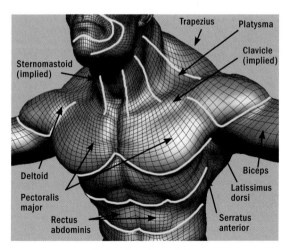

Neck and chest muscle flow

Note: *In the above image, the sternocleidomastoid is implied rather than built into the geometry. Instead, the platysma is built so you can create the fine pulling around the neck and chest during contraction.*

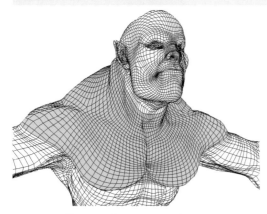

The cape - like geometry on the shoulders

To avoid geometry bunching up around the armpits, the beast's upper torso should be modeled a little differently than how it naturally flows. It is a good idea to have the edge loops flow along the pectoralis muscles into the deltoids and then to the back like a cape. This cape layout has the potential of deforming extremely well when the arms reach above the head and when they are in a relaxed position.

In the following image, there are many directional changes around the forearm, biceps and triceps. The trick is to try to build enough of these muscles without the arm being perfectly anatomically correct. Some areas are implied rather than built to keep the geometry efficient and uniformly spaced.

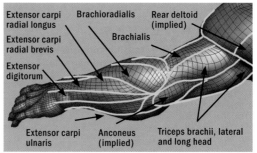

Arm muscle flow

Modeling the leg muscles is a good exercise for determining which muscles to build and what you can get away with. You can imply a good portion of the muscles just by sculpting with Artisan since most of the leg muscles travel vertically. Always evaluate what needs to be modeled and what does not. You should only concentrate on modeling what will pay off in the final render.

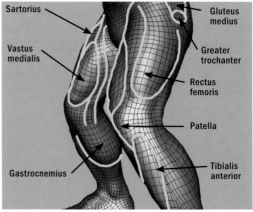

Legs muscle flow

> **Tip:** One of the biggest advantages of polygonal modeling is the ability to localize detail on a single surface mesh, which makes it ideal to work with when modeling organic characters.

Uniformly spaced geometry

The second key modeling concept covered here is spacing your geometry uniformly. This will give the most predictable surface possible when subdividing your creature's geometry. Subdividing can occur not only while modeling, but also when refining subdivision surfaces, when applying a *polySmooth,* or when the model is subdivided by the renderer at render time.

The advantages of having uniformly spaced geometry with a higher poly count are far greater than a mesh that has irregularly spaced geometry and less polygons. An evenly spaced geometry will also make the rest of the character pipeline much easier. Texture artists will experience a minimal amount of texture stretching on a surface that has uniform spacing compared to irregularly spaced geometry. Character set-up artists will have an easier time binding the model due to evenly distributed weight values to uniformly spaced geometry compared to geometry with irregularly spaced rows of edges.

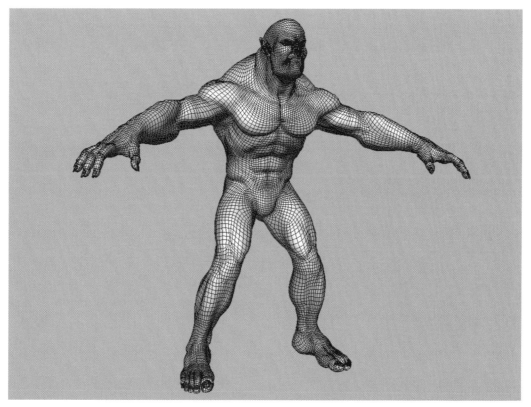

This project's creature is around 32,000 polygons

Quad topology

The third key modeling concept covered here is to maintain quad topology as much as possible. By doing so, it benefits you and everyone in the character pipeline for many of the same reasons as listed above. Quads benefits the modeler by getting a predictably smooth surface when subdivided, they benefit the texture artist by securing the texture placement and minimizing stretching and they allow the set-up artist to evenly distribute or paint weight values to quads rather than triangles or n-sided polygons.

There will be times when you will have to sacrifice one or more of these key concepts in order to maintain a quad layout, especially when modeling according to anatomy and muscle flow. It is then up to the modeler to decide to discontinue some of these extra edge loops by using triangles on the mesh.

Following are some typical topology problems encountered while modeling, along with solutions to correct the topology with quads. Once the topology is corrected, you can use tools such as Artisan to smooth out the edges and get a seamless result.

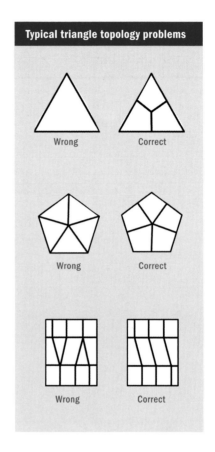

Typical triangle topology problems

Wrong   Correct

Wrong   Correct

Wrong   Correct

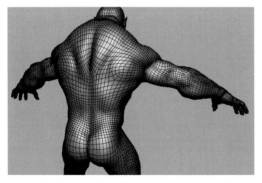

Try to always model creating quads

If you do have triangles on your model, make a conscious effort to hide them in unobtrusive places. N-sided polygons are not recommended either and should be split manually, since it is difficult to predict exactly how the surface will react when subdivided, textured or bounded; it might ultimately flicker when deforming during animation.

Conclusion

Ideally, you have spent some time planning and designing your character to be modeled. You should also have a good sense of how your character's muscles flow under the skin. Having a real sculpture on your desktop and reference pictures on your computer will be invaluable resources while modeling in 3D and will save you lots of time.

In the next lesson you will experiment in Maya software with some techniques for building your character.

Lesson 02 *Workflow*

Now that you have covered the first step of establishing and preparing your project, you can start looking into various tools and workflow techniques available in Maya software. Doing so will get you started in no time and will speed up your everyday tasks.

In this lesson you will learn the following:

- The Soft Modification Tool;

- How to use the Split Edge Ring Tool;

- How to use a MEL script to select edge rings;

- How to create custom hotkeys and Marking Menus.

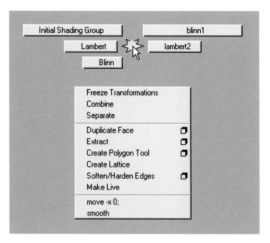

A custom Marking Menu

Soft Modification Tool

With the **Soft Modification Tool**, you can manipulate a group of vertices at the same time as a gradual fall-off from the deformer's center. This tool gives you the feeling of really sculpting in 3D, and is very handy with high resolution models. The following is a short description of how to use this tool.

1   Test geometry

- Select **Create** → **Polygon Primitives** → **Plane** → **❑**.

- **Scale** the geometry as desired.

Test geometry

2 Soft Modification Tool

You can use the Soft Modification Tool in two simple ways:

- With the plane still selected, click on the **Soft Modification Tool** icon in the **Toolbar**.

Or

- With the plane still selected, go to the **Animation** menu set by pressing **F2**, and select **Deform** → **Soft Modification**.

Once you use the tool, you should see the deformer's manipulator appear in the view panel on the plane.

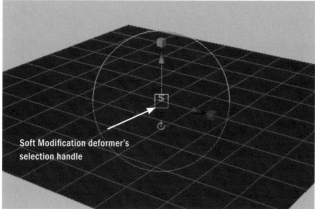

Soft Modification deformer's selection handle

The soft modification manipulator

Soft Modification Tool ──→

The Soft Modification Tool in the toolbar

Note: You can use the Soft Modification Tool on selected components to deform only a portion of a model, or select multiple objects to deform them all at once.

3 Deforming the surface

The deformer offers several attributes that will affect the geometry. Following are some general interest functionalities.

- Use the manipulator to transform the deformer (see diagram on next page).

- Click on the manipulator's **Cycling Index** to change the displayed manipulator.

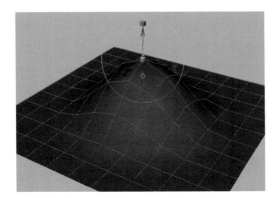

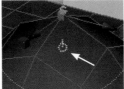

Sculpting a surface using the deformer *The manipulator's cycling index*

Doing so will toggle from the transform manipulator to the deformation manipulator.

- Move the manipulator to change the center of deformation.

- **Click+drag** on the outer circle to change the deformer's falloff or hold the **b** hotkey and **MMB-click+drag**.

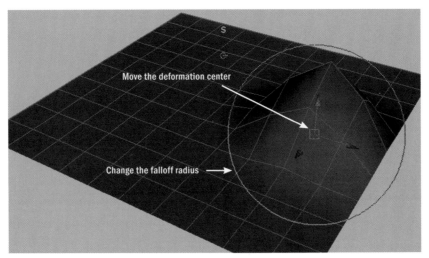

Changing the center of deformation and falloff

- Create another Soft Modification deformer, if desired.

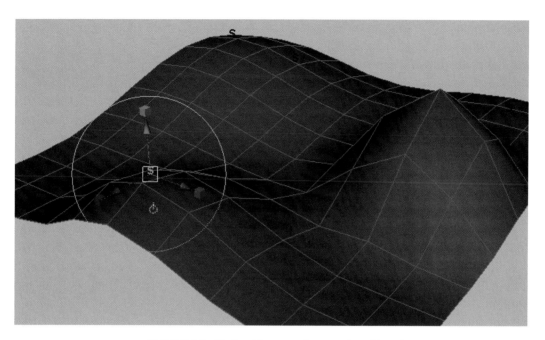

Multiple Soft Modification deformers on the same piece of geometry

> **Tip:** When the Soft Modification Tool is enabled, you just have to click on the surface to create a deformer at that location.

4 Construction history

When using the Soft Modification deformer, if the **Preserve History** option is turned **On**, a node will be created for each deformer that is visible in the Hypergraph or Outliner. These nodes can then be used as part of rigging or animation, as long as you keep the construction history on the model.

If the **Preserve History** option of the deformer is turned **Off**, you will be able to sculpt the geometry, but as soon as you deselect the deformer or create a new one, the deformation will be applied to the geometry and the deformer will be removed. This allows you to quickly sculpt the surface to your liking without having to bother with construction history.

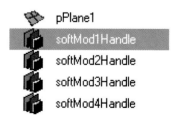

The deformers in the Outliner

5 Deleting deformers

If you wish to delete the deformer and remove its effect on the geometry, simply delete the deformer. On the other hand, if you want to delete the deformer but keep its effect on the model, you must select the model, then **Edit** → **Delete by Type** → **History**.

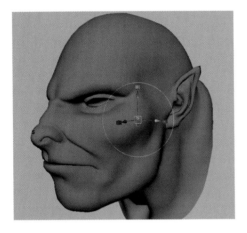

6 Deforming a head

- Open the file named *02-head.ma* from the *support_files*.

- Use the Soft Modification Tool to deform the head geometry.

- Double-click on the **Soft Modification Tool** in the toolbox and toggle the **Preserve History** option to see its effect when creating new deformers.

Movie: *The movie named 02-SoftModifications.avi in the support_files illustrates how to use the Soft Modification Tool.*

Edge rings and edge loops

An edge ring is a path of polygon edges that are connected in sequence by their shared faces. An edge loop is a continued line of polygonal edges that crosses a surface.

The **Split Edge Ring Tool** lets you select and then split polygon faces across either a full or partial edge ring on a polygonal mesh. This tool is useful when you want to add detail across a large area of a polygon mesh, but don't want to use the **Split Polygon Tool** to manually split every polygon face individually.

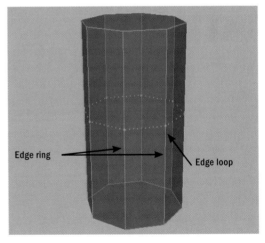

Edge ring and edge loop

Using the Split Edge Ring Tool

In the following example, you will use the tool on a primitive mesh in order to understand the tool's concepts and various usages.

1   Create a basic primitive

- Select **Create** → **Polygon Primitives** → **Plane** → ❑.

- Set the plane's **Subdivisions Width** and **Subdivisions Height** to **1**.

2   Split Edge Ring Tool

- From the **Modeling** menu set, select **Edit Polygons** → **Split Edge Ring Tool** → ❑.

- Make sure that **Auto Complete** is turned **On**.

- **Click+drag** on any of the edges of the plane to choose a splitting location, and then release the mouse button to execute the tool.

- **Click+drag** on another edge to split again.

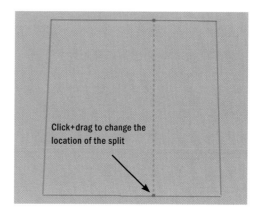

Click+drag to change the location of the split

Splitting from edge to edge

Note: *When you split across an edge ring, the split will be stopped if it encounters a poly face other than a four-sided one.*

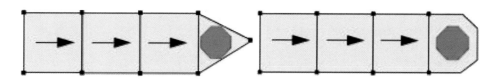

Triangles and n-sided polygons will stop the edge ring split

3   Construction history

Tweak the plane as follows:

- Select the **Split Edge Ring Tool** in the toolbox or press the **Y** hotkey.

- **Split** any vertical edge of the plane.

- Press the **Q** hotkey to **exit** the tool.

- Press the **F8** hotkey to go back into **Object mode**.

- With the plane selected, highlight the *polySplitRing* node in the **Inputs** section of the **Channel Box**.

Notice that construction history was conserved and that the split can still be modified.

- Highlight the **Weight** attribute and then **click+drag** with your **MMB** in the viewport.

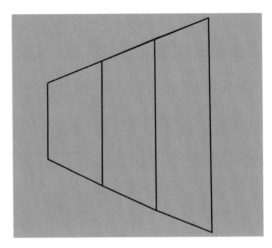

The reshaped plane with splits

Note: *You can change the location of the split interactively even after it is created.*

- Change **Absolute Weight** to **On**.

*A relative split will follow the shape of the mesh smoothly, while an absolute split will conserve an equal distance entirely along the closest edge. Changing the **Direction** attribute will make the split follow the opposite edge.*

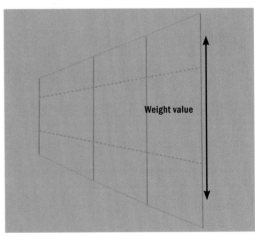

Changing the construction history of splits

> **Tip:**   Since construction history is conserved when using the **Split Edge Ring Tool**, you can change at anytime the values of a split and other splits will get updated accordingly. Consider deleting the model's construction history in order to lighten your scene.

Modeling tools

In order to help with your repetitive modeling tasks, you must be able to access tools in an optimized way to save as much time as possible. Tools that you might end up using a lot are called **Edge Ring Utilities** and **Edge Loop Utilities**, and they can be particularly handy when modeling in high resolution.

Do the following to access these tools and save them to your shelves. The tools can then be assigned to a hotkey and used seamlessly while working.

1   Select an edge ring

- In a new scene, **create** a **primitive polygonal sphere**.

- With the new sphere selected, press the **F10** hotkey to activate the edge selection mask.

- Select an edge.

- Hold down **Ctrl** and then **RMB-click** on the sphere.

Doing so will pop up a contextual menu.

- Select **Edge Ring Utilities** → **To Edge Ring.**

The tool selects all the edges along the same polygonal ring, until it hits a triangle or an n-sided polygon. In this case, if you selected a vertical edge, you selected the entire edge ring around the sphere. If you selected a horizontal edge, then the selection stops at the poles of the sphere.

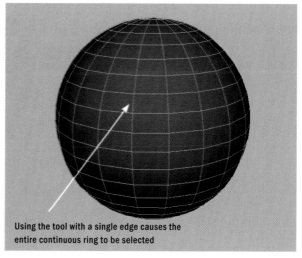

Using the tool with a single edge causes the entire continuous ring to be selected

Using ringSelect

2   The Script Editor

Alternatively, you can retrieve the tool's command through the Script Editor and then save it to your shelf.

- Select **Windows** → **General Editors**→ **Script Editor**.

- In the Script Editor, turn **On** the **Script** → **Echo All Commands** option.

- **Redo** the last step in order to see the MEL command used.

Doing so display all the hidden commands executed, thus giving you access to the **SelectEdgeRing** *command.*

- Make sure to turn **Off** the **Script** → **Echo All Commands** option when you are done.

- If you want, you can highlight and **MMB-click+drag** the command to your shelf for later usage.

Hotkeys

When you become specialized in a certain module of Maya software, such as modeling, you will surely devise your own way of working. Most of the time, this involves custom hotkeys. Hotkeys significantly help to speed up your workflow and should be considered whenever working with Maya.

The following example will show you an example of how to create a custom hotkey.

Tip: *If you are new to modeling or new to Maya, it is recommended to first memorize where each tool is located in the default Maya settings. Once you are comfortable with the default hotkeys, you can begin to implement new custom hotkeys.*

1   Bring up the Hotkey Editor

- Select **Windows** → **Settings/Preferences** → **Hotkeys**.

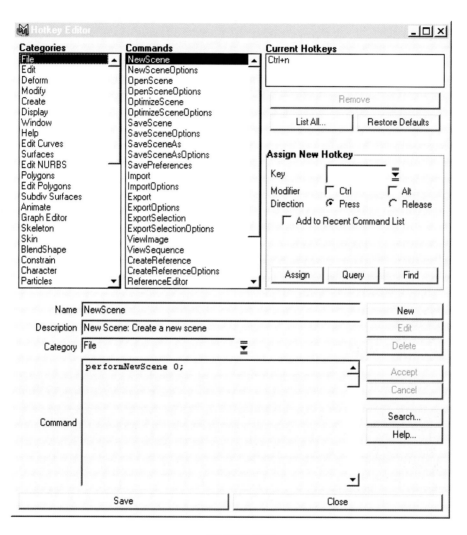

The Hotkey Editor

2   Creating a custom hotkey

- Click the **New** button to create a new hotkey.

- Fill in the hotkey fields as follows:

    Name to *ringSelect*;

    Description to *Invoke the SelectEdgeRing command.*

- Set **Category** to **User**.

- In the **Command** field, enter the following MEL command:

    SelectEdgeRing;

- Click the **Accept** button.

The new ringSelectHotkey command is now listed under the **User** *category in the top portion of the Hotkey Editor.*

3   Assign the hotkey

- Highlight the *ringSelectHotkey* command in the **Commands** section.

- Under the **Assign New Hotkey** section, set your desired hotkey, such as **Ctrl+j**.

Notice the informational message that specifies that this hotkey was not previously assigned to any other command. This is what you want in order to not overwrite another useful hotkey.

- Once you make your choice for a good hotkey, click the **Assign** button.

You will notice that the hotkey is listed in the **Current Hotkeys** *section for the highlighted command.*

4   Save your preferences

- Click on the **Save** button at the bottom of the **Hotkey Editor**.

Doing so will save your preferences, keeping your custom hotkey in a new Maya session.

- Click on the **Close** button to dismiss the **Hotkey Editor**.

5   Try out your new hotkey

Marking Menus

Hotkeys allow you to assign a command per key and you might eventually completely fill the keyboard with custom commands. A solution for this is to open the **Marking Menu Editor** and create Marking Menus. This way, you can gather several of your custom commands under a single Marking Menu.

Marking Menus can be accessed in two different ways. One is to assign the Marking Menu to a hotkey through the Hotkey Editor, which is what you will see here. The other way is to access the Marking Menu through the Hotbox, via the spacebar.

> **Movie:** *You can also watch the movie called 02-MarkingMenus.avi from the support_files to see how to create Marking Menus.*

1   Marking Menu Editor

- Select **Windows** → **Settings/Preferences** → **Marking Menus**.

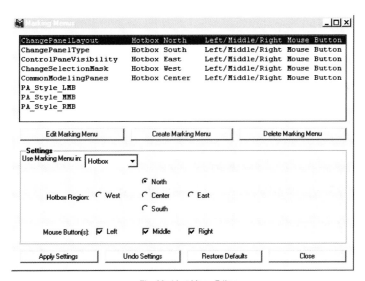

The Marking Menu Editor

2   Create a Marking Menu

- Click the **Create Marking Menu** button.

Doing so will pop the Create Marking Menu window.

- Enter a proper name in the **Menu Name** field, such as *ModelingMenu*.

3   Populating the Marking Menu

In order to add items to your Marking Menu, you must add scripts to the different boxes of the menu. To do so, you can either **MMB-click+drag** scripts from your shelves to the appropriate boxes or **right-click** on a box and select **Edit Menu Item**.

4   Test and save the Marking Menu

To test your Marking Menu, click in the test area at the bottom of the window. Once you are satisfied with it, click the **Save** and **Close** buttons.

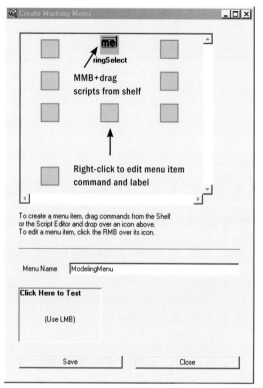

Assign commands to the new Marking Menu

5   Make the Marking Menu available to the Hotkey Editor

When you return to the Marking Menu Editor, you should see your new *ModelingMenu* highlighted.

- With the Marking Menu highlighted, set **Use Marking Menu** in the **Hotkey Editor**.

An informational message tells you that the Marking Menu will be available in the Hotkey Editor.

- Click the **Apply Settings** button, then the **Close** button.

6 Assign the Marking Menu to a hotkey

- Open the Hotkey Editor.

- Highlight the **User Marking Menu** category, then highlight the *ModelingMenu_Press* command.

- **Assign** an appropriate hotkey to the command, such as **Ctrl+j**.

*Doing so will replace the previously created hotkey with the new custom Marking Menu. When assigning the Marking Menu hotkey, click **Yes** to automatically set-up the release hotkey for the Marking Menu.*

- Click the **Save** and **Close** button to dismiss the Hotkey Editor.

7 Test your Marking Menu

- Select a polygonal edge.

- **Press and hold** the hotkey set in the previous step.

- Click in the viewport to invoke the Marking Menu and select the proper command.

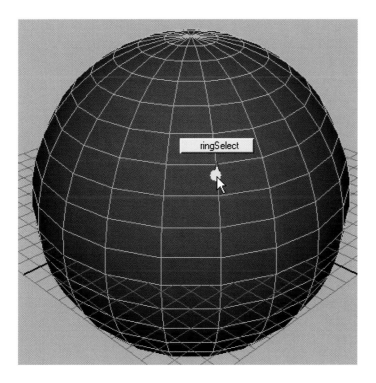

The custom Marking Menu is displayed

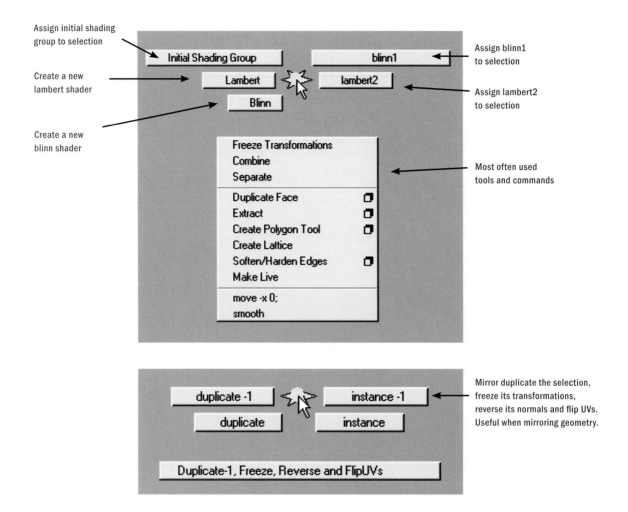

Assign initial shading group to selection

Create a new lambert shader

Create a new blinn shader

Assign blinn1 to selection

Assign lambert2 to selection

Most often used tools and commands

Mirror duplicate the selection, freeze its transformations, reverse its normals and flip UVs. Useful when mirroring geometry.

Tip: *It is also possible to customize Marking Menus even more, but doing so involves advance scripting skills, which will not be covered here.*

Conclusion

In this lesson, you have seen how to use basic Maya tools, MEL scripts, hotkeys and Marking Menus, which are all components of your everyday tasks. Being able to fully integrate these subjects will, without a doubt, speed up your workflow and save you a tremendous amount of time in the end.

In the next lesson, you will model the beast. Keep in mind that it is up to you to customize the Maya software interface to your liking.

Lesson 03 *Modeling*

You will now begin modeling the beast. To do so, you will start by importing reference images in Maya software and then blocking out the character. Once that is done, you will be able to refine the beast by gradually increasing its geometry and using some simple tricks to generate a good topology.

In this lesson you will learn the following:

- What a default pose is;

- How to import image planes;

- How to block out a character;

- How to increase resolution;

- Tricks to help modeling.

The final beast model

Default pose

A default pose is the pose given to a character when modeled. This pose will then be used everywhere else in the pipeline. For instance, the texture artist will start from this pose to unfold UVs and the rigging artist will start from this pose to rig and skin the character.

A character's default pose should aesthetically reflect your creature's attitude and weight. The beast modeled in this book is very top-heavy, and if you model it with its back straight without the natural S-curve in its spine or with its arms completely straight, it would not look very natural. If your creature does not look natural at its default pose, chances are it will not look natural when it is deformed.

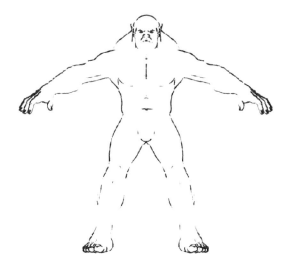

The beast's default pose

Thinking about the deformation of a model at the rigging stage, the default pose should have articulations bent halfway between its maximum and minimum bending angle. This is because you want as little articulation deformation as possible on any part of the body. For instance, if you model the elbow at its maximum opening angle, the geometry will look good when the arm is opened, but chances are that the geometry will be squashed when the arm is closed. The same thing would happen if you model the elbow in a completely closed position. So your best bet in order to have a well deforming character is to model it in a relaxed position, without extreme stretching or bending.

A character's default pose is also very important to establish when considering your project's specific needs. For instance, if you want to apply any simulations to your creature, such as cloth, you should consider modeling your creature's arms out to the side and its legs spaced out slightly more than you would normally stand. Such simulations generally work best when there is no intersecting geometry.

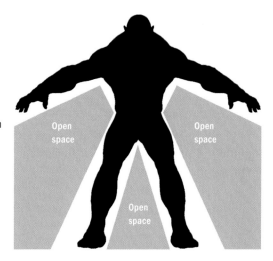

Open spaces between limbs to help dynamic simulation

Image planes

One of the benefits of spending time designing your model before beginning in 3D is that you can draw reference images to establish proportions while in default pose. Doing so helps model the character, since the poses can be displayed using image planes in the Maya viewport.

Following are three reference images that will be used to model the beast. Notice that they are proportionate altogether in order to facilitate the modeling while looking through the different Orthographic views.

1 Start a new scene

You will now import the front, side and top reference images as image planes in Maya software.

- Select **File → New Scene**.

Do not manipulate any of the cameras.

2 Importing the image planes

- In the *Perspective* view, select **Panels → Saved Layouts → Four View**.

- In the *front* view, select **View → Image Plane → Import Image…**

Doing so will open a dialog box to browse for the image plane.

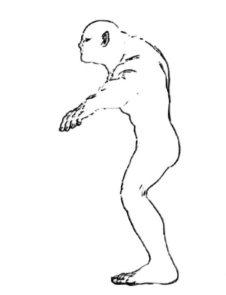

- Select the image *beast_front.tif* from the support files and click the **Open** button.

The image plane is shown in the front view.

- **Repeat** the previous steps to import the *beast_top.tif* and *beast_side.tif* images for their respective cameras.

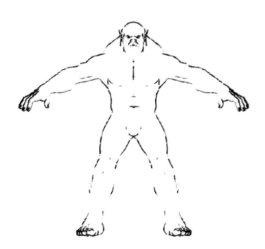

Modeling reference image planes

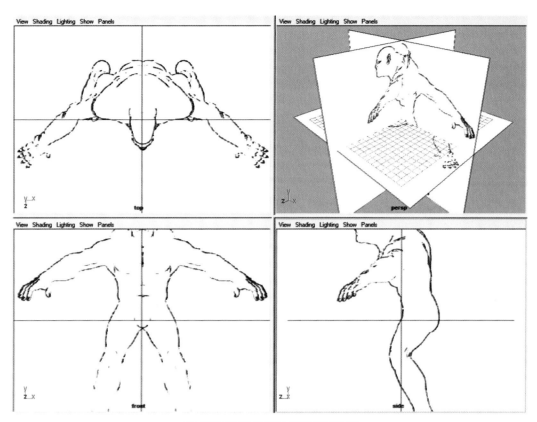

The image planes for each Orthographic view

3   Placing the image planes

Now that you have the image planes in your scene, you will need to place them correctly in order to be able to start modeling.

- In the *front* view, select **View** → **Image Plane** → **Image Plane Attributes** → **imagePlane1**.

The Attribute Editor will display the image plane's attributes.

- Under the **Placement Extras** section, set **Center Z** to **-20**.

- Set the *top* view's image plane's **Center Y** to **-20**.

- Set the *side* view's image plane's **Center X** to **-20**.

Tip: *If you save your reference images with an Alpha channel, they can be displayed in the viewports with transparency, which can be very useful while modeling. This will display lines only in the viewport, so it is not always necessary to offset the planes from the center of origin.*

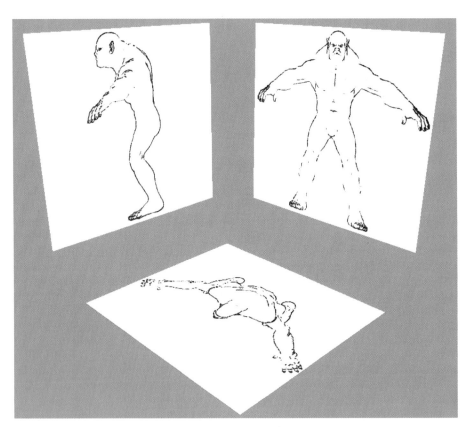

The image planes in Maya software

Tip: The convention is to always model your character facing the Z-positive axis, as shown here. It is up to you to determine if you need to offset or scale the image planes to suit this rule.

4   Save your work

Blocking

Perhaps one of the most common ways to begin modeling is by blocking the basic shape of the character, starting from a primitive polygonal cube, and then building up until a decent shape is achieved.

1   Scene file

- Continue with our own scene file.

Or

- Open the scene file *03-imagePlanes.ma*.

2   Create a polygon cube

- Select **Create** → **Polygon Primitives** → **Cube**.

The properly placed cube

- **Rename** *pCube1* to *beastGeo*.

- With the *beastGeo* selected, set the *polyCube1*'s **Subdivisions Width** to **2** in the Channel Box.

- From the *front* and *side* views, **scale** and **move** the *beastGeo* to fit the pelvis of the beast in the image planes.

> **Tip:**   It is a good idea to enable the Wireframe on Shaded and X-Ray options from the view's Shading menu.

3   Start blocking the torso

You can now begin blocking the beast using basic Maya tools.

- With the cube selected, press the **F11** hotkey to enable the poly face selection mask.

- Select the two top faces of the cube.

- Make sure the **Polygons** → **Tool Options** → **Keep New Faces Together** option is turned **On**.

This option ensures extracted faces are extracted as a group rather than as individual faces. Select **Edit Polygons** → **Extrude Face***.*

- Move the extruded faces up.

> **Tip:**   Press the **G** hotkey to invoke the last tool used, in this case, the **Extrude Face Tool**.

- Continue extruding in order to form the beast's torso and head.

Make sure to keep the geometry simple at this stage; your goal is only to achieve a good basic shape.

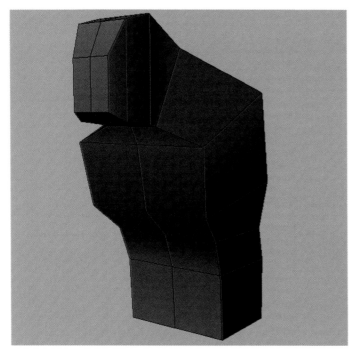

The beast's blocked torso

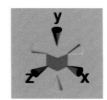

The View Compass

Note: Don't forget to look through other views to ensure you are following the image planes correctly. If you don't want to repeatedly switch cameras, you can use the **View Compass** in the upper right corner of the Perspective view. This tool can be used to quickly change to Orthographic views.

4   Mirrored instance

A good trick to use when modeling a symmetrical character is to use a mirrored instance. Since you increased the width subdivisions of the cube in **Step 2**, it is now easy to delete half of the model and create a mirrored instance.

Tip: If you prefer to model your geometry as one single mesh, you can skip this step and use the **Reflection** option of the **Move Tool**, which allows you to translate components on both sides of a model at once.

- Select all the faces on the right side of the beast's torso and **delete** them.

- Back in Object mode, select the *beastGeo* and select **Edit** → **Duplicate** → ❏.

- In the Duplicate options, set the following:

  Scale X to **-1**;

  Geometry Type to **Instance**.

- Click the **Duplicate** button.

A mirrored piece of geometry is created. Since this is an instance, any modifications made to the original beastGeo mesh will also be made onto its instance.

5   Save your work

- Save your scene as *03-blocking_01.ma*.

Movie: *Watch the movie called blocking.mov to see how to block the beast.*

6   Extrude the arms and legs

Using the common polygonal tools, such as **Extrude Face**, **Split Edge Ring** and **Split Polygon**, extrude the beast's arm and leg and define its overall shape.

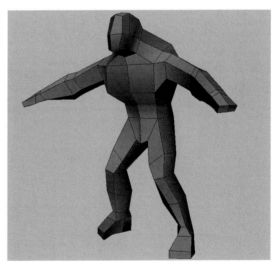

The arms and legs extruded

Note: *You should NOT be modeling facial, finger or toe details at this stage.*

7   Save your work

- Save your scene as *03-blocking_02.ma*.

8   Increase the overall level of detail

Gradually increase the definition of the
existing geometry in order to remove any
coarse-looking polygons.

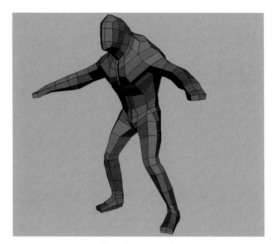

The refined geometry

Tip: Try to not move the central vertices away from their mirror axis since that would create a
gap between the geometry and its instance. If you do move the central vertices, simply snap
them back to the central axis.

Note: You should now have at least one edge ring per articulation, such as knee, ankle, elbow,
wrist, etc.

9   Sculpting the model

Use the Edit Polygons → Sculpt Geometry Tool to sculpt the geometry to your liking by pushing,
pulling and smoothing vertices.

10 Save your work

- Save your scene as *03-blocking_03.ma*.

Tip: If you hold down the **u** hotkey and **LMB-click**, you can access a menu that will allow you to
quickly switch the painting operation. You can also create your own custom Marking Menu
to set the tool's options in the viewport rather than in the tool window.

Adding details

Now that you have a basic geometry with good proportions, you can start thinking about modeling details such as muscles, fingers, toes and face. For the fingers, you will only have to model the thumb and one finger to duplicate the others and attach them to complete the hand. The same idea will be used for the toes.

1 Scene file

- Open the scene file *03-details_01.ma*.

In this scene, the body was refined and the face, thumb, one finger and two toes were also modeled.

2 Create an opening for the duplicated fingers

Since you will be creating the other fingers by duplicating the index of the beast, you will need to create openings at the tip of the palm.

- **Select** and **delete** the faces to create openings for the new fingers.

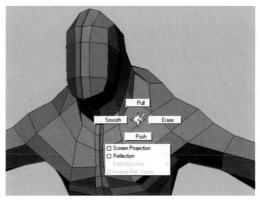

The paint operation menu

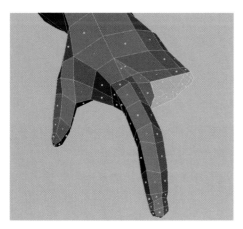

The deleted faces

Details modeled

3 Duplicate the fingers

- Select the faces of the index.

- Select **Edit Polygons → Duplicate Face → ▢**.

- In the Duplicate Face option window, turn **Off** the Separate Duplicate Faces, then click the Duplicate button.

Doing so will duplicate the selected faces and keep them part of the original mesh.

- **Scale** and **move** the duplicated finger to be the middle finger.

- Repeat for the remaining fingers.

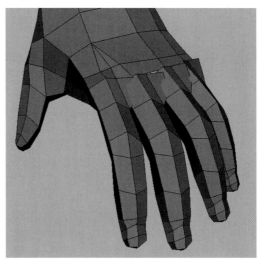

The duplicated fingers

4 Combine the geometry

- Select all the geometry.

- Select **Edit → Delete All by Type → History**.

- Select **Polygons → Combine**.

Doing so will combine the different polygonal shells into a single mesh.

5 Attach the fingers

- Select an open vertex at the base of the new fingers.

- Hold down **v** to enable **Snap to Point**.

- Snap the vertex to the desired location on the palm's opening.

- Use the **Split Polygon Tool** if you need to add vertices to the palm for snapping.

- Repeat the previous steps to close all the openings of the palm with the fingers.

- Once all the gaps between the fingers and the palm are closed, select the beastGeo, then select **Edit Polygons → Merge Vertices**.

Doing so will combine the vertices that were snapped together, thus creating a single mesh without holes or seams.

6 Repeat for the toes

Use the same technique as shown above to duplicate and attach the toes.

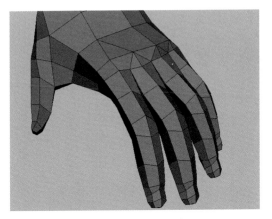

The combined and attached fingers

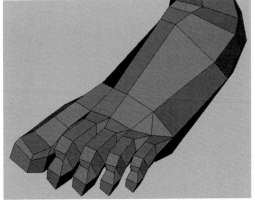

The combined and attached toes

7 Delete the image planes

At this stage, you can delete the image planes, since you should be done modeling the general shape of the character.

- In the Hypershade, select the **Cameras** tab.

- **Delete** the three image planes created earlier.

8 Scale the beast

You can now establish the beast's height and overall scale by using the *Measurement Tool*. The beast should be huge, so its height should be roughly 254 centimeters (100 inches) tall. It is important to establish the scale of your creature early on.

> **Note:** *Everyone throughout the pipeline will depend on this height/scale so you want to be sure that it will not change.*

- **Duplicate** an instanced mirror of the beast geometry to see its overall shape.

- **Translate** the beast geometry in order to plant the feet on the Perspective grid.

- Press the **Insert** key to enter the pivot mode.

- Hold down **x** to snap the pivot of the beast at the origin.

- Press **Insert** again to exit pivot mode.

- Select **Create** → **Measure Tools** → **Distance Tool**.

- From the *side* view, press **x** to snap to grid and click at the origin to create the first measurement locator.

- Still holding **x**, snap the second measurement locator anywhere along the **Y-axis**.

- Select the top locator and set its **Translate Y** to **254**.

Note: Make sure that **Working Units** in the Maya preferences are set to **centimeter**.

- Select the geometry and **scale** it up uniformly until its head reaches **254 units** high.

The Measure Tool

9   Clean up

- With the *beastGeo* still selected, select **Modify** → **Freeze Transformations**.

This will reset the transformation attributes of the geometry to their default value. From now on, the beastGeo should always stay at this default position and scaling.

- Select **Edit** → **Delete by Type** → **History**.

Any construction history that remains on the geometry is now cleaned up.

- You can now delete the locators and measurement node.

> **Tip:** *Use Edit Polygons → Normals → Soften/Harden to smooth the normals of your model.*

10 Save your work

- Save your scene as *03-details_02.ma*.

Analyzing the silhouette

When modeling or sculpting, you should always keep in mind the silhouette of your creature. Analyzing the silhouette of your geometry can be extremely helpful since the brain does an abstraction of what the model looks like and concentrates on its shape, form, proportions and eventually rhythm when animated. The following shows you how to view the silhouette of your model directly in Maya software.

1 Lighting mode

- Press **7** on your keyboard or select **Lighting** → **Use All Lights** in the desired view panel.

Doing so will turn on the hardware lighting of your scene. Since there are no lights in the scene, the models are black.

2 Analyze the model

- Move your model around and **zoom** out in order to get a good sense of its shape.

- Tweak the model as needed.

- When you are done, press **5** on your keyboard to turn off hardware lighting.

Model silhouettes

Increasing resolution

You can now begin increasing the resolution of the model in order to achieve the best definition of the beast. Keep in mind that you should achieve as much detail as you can by using the fewest possible polygons or edge rings. This workflow does not use a lower resolution proxy to produce the high resolution model. By creating every edge manually, you have *complete control* over the topology and polygon count of your mesh instead of getting the geometry to a certain resolution and then smoothing it.

The main tools used in this step should be the **Split Polygon Tool** and the **Split Edge Ring Tool**.

> **Tip:** You should also extensively use the panoply of very useful modeling commands found under the contextual menu accessed by pressing ***Ctrl-Click+LMB*** on the geometry.

In order to prevent the Split Edge Ring Tool from splitting up the entire model all at once and localizing your edits, you might want to turn off the Auto Complete option of the tool. This allows you to specify from which to which polygonal edges you want to split along. Another workflow is to divide your model into sections such as the head, torso, arms, legs, hands and feet, in order to be able to really focus on the portion of the model that you are working on.

Increasing the overall definition of the beast

Splitting polygons

Modeling edge loops that flow with the muscles can be a time-consuming process and there is no quick and easy way of achieving this.

When you first begin a model, you usually need to block all the important edge rings, up to the point where you can begin splitting edges to match muscle flow. You can then concentrate on creating important definition to the edge rings. At this point, you don't need to bother keeping everything in quads. Quads become important once the definition of the entire character is established.

Following are some example techniques that can be used to help create the muscle flow.

1   Guide curves

When your topology is flowing in different directions than what it should be, it can be difficult to break away from it. A recommended technique is to draw NURBS curves on the surface of the creature, which can serve as helpful guides when modeling according to your creature's muscle flow. These curves are then referred to as guide curves.

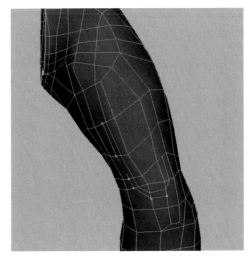

Splitting according to muscle flow

- Select the geometry for which you wish to create guide curves.

- Toggle **On** the **Make Live** button located in the Status Line or select **Modify** → **Make Live**.

- Select **Create** → **EP Curve Tool**.

- Draw directly on the surface to create a guide curve that follows the shape of the live geometry.

- Assign the curves to a layer and then set a color override for that layer.

- Model the muscle flow of the geometry.

Note: *Coloring the curves will help you easily differentiate them from the geometry.*

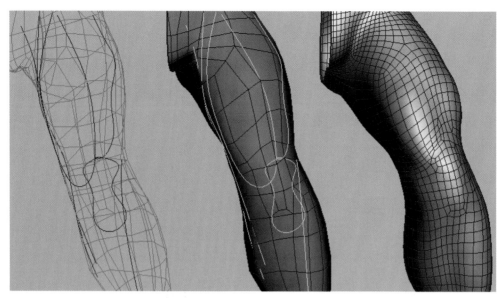

Using guide curves

2   Coloring row of faces

Once you have created a row of faces that define the muscles, it's helpful to apply a different color to the row as a visual guide when modeling.

You can do this easily by using the **ringSelect** command assigned to your Marking Menu in the previous lesson.

- Select an edge defining a row of modeled faces.

- Hold down **Ctrl**, then **RMB-click** on the geometry to choose **Edge Ring Utilities** → **To Edge Ring**.

Doing so will select all the edges that are part of that same row of faces.

- Convert the selection to faces by pressing **Ctrl+F11**.

- Apply a different colored shader to the row of faces.

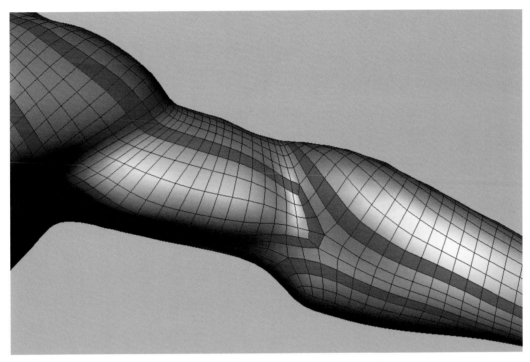

Colored face rows used as visual guides of defined muscles

Facial definition

Once you reach this point, you can start matching the likeness of the face to your original concept drawing and maquette. This is a very important step to be taken seriously, since the head is usually the focal point of a character.

In this section, you will experiment with techniques using the pictures of the maquette or concept drawings you made.

1   Set-up a new camera and image plane

- Select **Create** → **Cameras** → **Camera**.

- Rename the new camera to *modelingRefCam*.

- Select **Panels** → **Perspective** → **modelingRefCam** to make the new camera the active view.

- Select **View** → **Camera Settings** → **Resolution Gate**.

- Position the *modelingRefCam* to frame the face of the beast.

- Select **View** → **Image Plane** → **Import Image…**

- Browse for *beast.1.tif* from the support files and **import** it.

- Move the camera to roughly fit the head geometry with the image plane.

In order to be able to use multiple image planes without having to create other cameras, you can use the **Use Image Sequence** attribute of the image plane to change the image on different frames. You also need to set keyframes on the camera in order to adjust the view angle to fit the new image planes.

The geometry placed to fit the reference image

Tip: *If the image plane intersects with the beast geometry, simply increase the Depth attribute in the Channel Box for the image plane.*

Movie: *Refer to the movie 03-ImportingImagePlanes.avi to see how this is done.*

2 Zoomerate.mel

When modeling using image planes on a camera, you cannot move closer to your model, since that would offset the geometry and its image plane. In order to be able to zoom in and model without moving the *modelingRefCam*, you can employ a simple MEL script that uses the horizontal and vertical film offsets in conjunction with overscan.

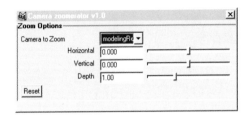

The zoomerator window

- Copy the *zoomerate.mel* script to your *scripts* folder and source it.

A window will appear, allowing you to control the specified camera.

3 Projected guide texture

Another good trick when modeling using image planes is to project the image onto the geometry as a texture.

Note: *When projecting image on geometry, the sides of the object will appear stretched. This is the reason why you will be projecting textures from different angles on the beast's head.*

Here is how you can do this:

- **Assign** a new **Lambert** material to the head geometry.

- In the Attribute Editor for the material, click on the **map** button for the *color channel*.

- In the Create Render Node window, select **As projection**, then create a **File** node.

- Back in the Attribute Editor for the *projection* node, under the **Projection Attributes** section, set **Proj Type** to **Perspective**.

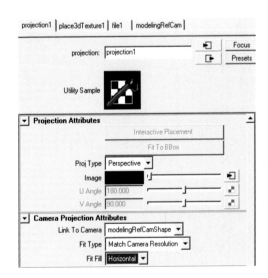

Setting the attributes of the projection node

- Set the following under the **Camera Projection Attributes** section:

  Fit Type to **Match Camera Resolution**;

  Link To Camera to **modelingRefCamShape**;

  Fit Fill to the same value used on the *modelingRefCam* image plane.

- For the file node, **browse** for the same image seen in the *modelingRefCam*, in this case *beast.1.tif*.

- Within the Perspective view, press the **6** hotkey to display hardware texturing.

You should now see the image plane being projected as a texture on the head geometry.

 Tip: *If the hardware texture is displayed at too low a resolution, select the material and set Texture Resolution under the Hardware Texturing section to Highest (256x256).*

- You can now start modeling details on the geometry, using the texture as a guide.

The image projected on the model as a reference

 Note: *When moving the geometry vertices, the texture will not update on its own. You must update it manually simply by right-clicking on the file node in the Hypershade and selecting Reload Image File.*

4 Refine the facial geometry as needed

You can now refer to your image planes
to refine the facial topology of the beast.
You can also model the teeth, the tongue
and the eyes.

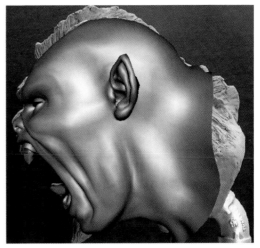

The facial details modeled using the image planes

Tip: *You can duplicate the head and use the Make Live Tool to create reference curves just
like in the previous lesson to help you with following the lines shown in the texture.*

Movie: *The scene with the camera and images set up is 03-facialDefinition.ma.*

> **Note:**   *It is up to you to model the face of the beast with its mouth open or closed. If modeling it open, ensure you have enough geometry to achieve this extreme pose. You will then be able to close the mouth at the end of the modeling process and use the open shape as a blend shape.*

Completing the model

You should have a well-defined model at this stage. It is now time to mirror duplicate and combine all the different pieces of the beast together. This step requires some work in order to have a good flowing topology from piece to piece, which will be explored in the next lesson.

You should complete the model with other objects such as the fingernails and toenails. When you are done, have a last look at the general shape of your character and tweak it as needed.

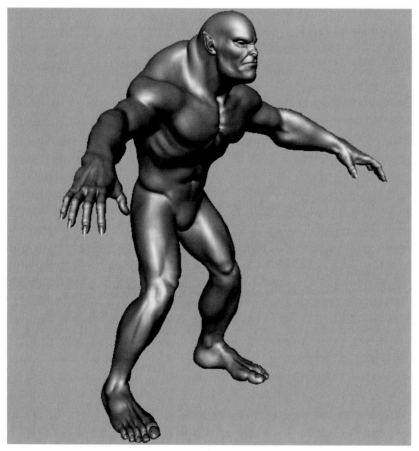

The combined beast geometry

Conclusion

You have now completed the task of modeling an entire character. Well done! You might find this process to be quite long, but it is actually a simple process with few tools to comprehend. As you gain experience in modeling, you will make fewer time-consuming errors. You will also be able to envision the exact topology that you need to achieve.

In the next lesson, you will review some ways of cleaning up the beast's topology.

Lesson 04 *Final Touches*

There are always improvements to bring to a model. This lesson will explore some workflow tips and tricks for making your model's topology as great as possible.

In this lesson you will learn the following:

- How to clean the topology;

- Where to hide triangles;

- Polishing the model;

- Final checklist.

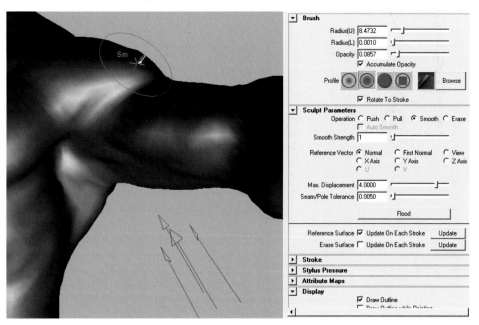

Using the Paint Geometry Tool

Cleaning the topology

You will now examine the beast's topology and locate areas that do not flow with the muscles, are not evenly spaced and which may contain n-sided faces or triangles.

Since the model's pieces were combined in the last lesson, it takes some planning to figure out how to properly merge these meshes together to form one clean model.

You will now look at a typical technique used for cleaning up a model.

> **Movie**: *Watch the movie called cleaningTopology.mov from the support files to see how this is done.*

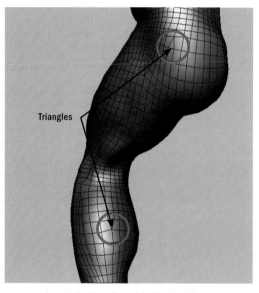
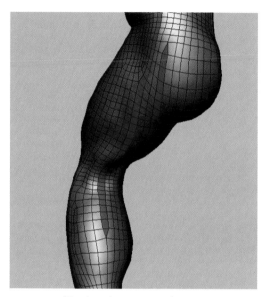

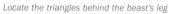

Locate the triangles behind the beast's leg

Triangles exist on separate face rows

1 Scene file

- Open the scene file *04-cleanup_01.ma*.

This file contains a leg of the beast with a typical triangle problem behind the leg.

2 Color the face rows

- **Create** a new **Lambert** shader in the Hypershade and set its **Color** to **red**.

- Select one edge per vertical face row containing the problematic triangles.

- Hold down **Ctrl** then **RMB-click** on the geometry.

- Select **To Face Path** in order to select the faces of the selected edge ring.

- Assign the red lambert to the selected faces.

3   Collapse edges

- Select a single edge on the first face row and select **Edit Polygons** → **Collapse**.

4   Collapse the lower row of faces

- Select a single edge in the lower red row of faces.

- Hold down **Ctrl** then **RMB-click** on the geometry.

- Select **Edge Ring Utilities** → **To Edge Ring and Collapse**.

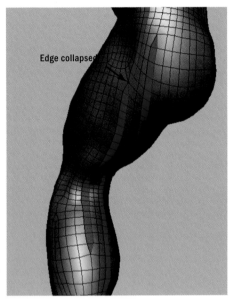

Collapse a single edge closer to the other triangle

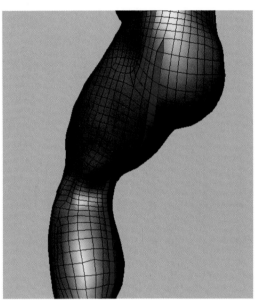

Row of edges collapsed together, thus moving the problem up

5   Bringing the triangles closer together

- Select edges in the row between the two red rows and collapse them in order to bring the two triangles even closer.

- Delete the edge at the bottom of the first row in order to create a quad, as shown in the picture.

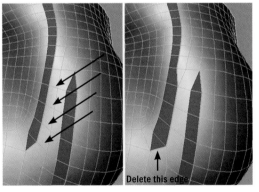

Edges to collapse

6   Remove the problem

Now that the two problematic triangles are side by side, you can simply use the **Split Polygon Tool** and delete the triangle edges to correct the problem.

7   Smoothing the surface

In order to remove all traces of the correction you just made to the model, use the **Sculpt Geometry Tool** to smooth out the polygons.

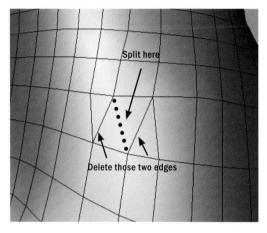

Smoothed geometry

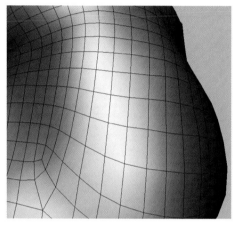

Problem solved

Hiding triangles

In almost any case, you will have triangles in your model. Since you cannot get rid of all of them, it is recommended to at least hide them as much as you can.

> **Note:**   *Triangles may cause texture stretching and flickering and they are harder to skin properly.*

The following images show places where you can safely hide triangles. Obviously, this will differ from model to model, so use your best judgment. A good rule is to hide them where they won't be easily noticeable and in places that do not deform much.

- Consider hiding your triangles in the back and the neck. This is especially true if your character has hair. You can also hide triangles around the rear deltoid.

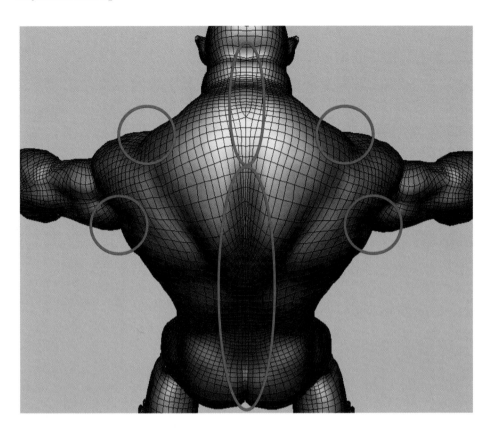

- The pit of the neck, the armpit and the inner part of the wrist are good places to hide triangles.

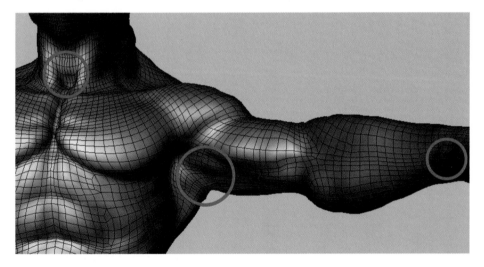

- The feet, the groin and the calves are ideal places to hide triangles.

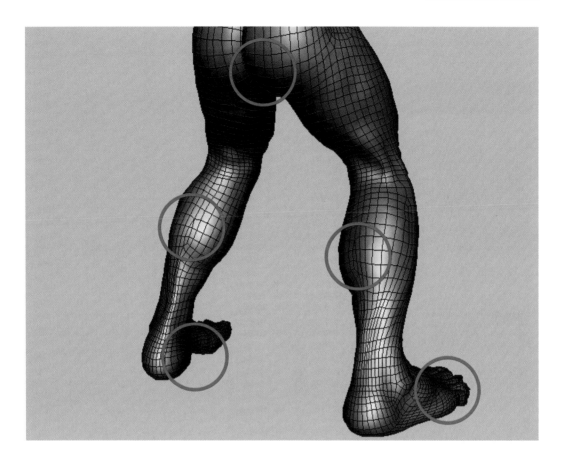

Polishing the model

This should be the last stage. Now that you have covered all of the technical issues regarding edge rings and topology, you can concentrate solely on the aesthetics. The best way to polish the model is to use the **Sculpt Geometry Tool** to push, pull and smooth the geometry. This is a perfect tool at this stage because it really gives you the feeling of sculpting in 3D.

Looking at your model using hardware lighting

While refining the surface with the Sculpt Tool, it is a good idea to examine how the light affects the surface. To do so, do the following:

- **Assign** a **Blinn** material to your geometry.

- Create a directional light.

- Press **7** on your keyboard to enable the hardware lighting.

- **Rotate** the light to find areas that may not be as organic as you would like and smooth them out.

When rotating a directional light in your scene, you can discover many areas on your model that still need refinement.

Hardware lighting

Final checklist

Before you can pass the model off to the texture artists and character set-up artists, you must first make sure the scene follows some basic criteria:

- The hierarchy of models is well organized and will remain in a consistent order throughout the pipeline.

- All geometry in the scene has a unique name following a naming convention.

- All geometry has frozen transformations.

- All history has been deleted via the **Edit** → **Delete All by Type** → **History** command.

- All geometry has the default lambert shader assigned.

- All extraneous nodes have been removed via the **File** → **Optimize Scene Size** command.

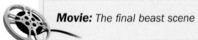

Movie: *The final beast scene file is 04-BeastFinal.ma in the support_file/scenes folder.*

Conclusion

The methods discussed thus far in the modeling steps of the beast are a compilation of many tests and experiments to find the most versatile mesh possible. This is, by no means, the definitive way of modeling a character. A subject can be approached in a number of different ways for modeling anatomy, which can lead to completely different models. Your working technique will be constantly changing and evolving due to the specific needs of each project, and not just the underlying muscles, skeleton, tendons and skin deformations of your creature. There will always be trade-offs, but it all comes down to achieving a good model in the most efficient way possible. You should consider talking with animators and character set-up artists to ascertain how they envision the creature moving and deforming. These discussions will play a huge part in the way you approach the model.

In the next lesson you will experiment with unfolding UVs and texturing the beast.

Lesson 05 *Texturing*

Once a model is finished and ready to go on to the next stage, chances are that the texture artist will have to unfold UVs and paint textures for the model. There are several ways of unfolding UVs, so this lesson is intended only as an introduction.

In this lesson you will learn the following:

- How to project UVs;
- How to cut UVs;
- How to select contiguous edges;
- How to unfold UVs;
- How to export a UV snapshot;
- How to create a PSD network.

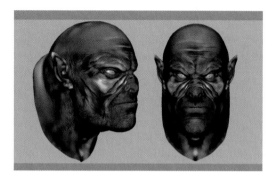

The unfolded head with texture

Project UVs

The first thing to do when you want to texture your character is to put some order in the UVs of your model. Usually, when you finish modeling, the UVs are completely disorganized. This is because you started modeling from a basic primitive and have extracted, split and deleted several edges. Projecting UVs will give you a good starting point to unfold the model.

1 Scene file

- Continue from your own scene file.

Or

- Open the scene file *05-texture_01.ma*.

2 UV Editor

- Select the beast model.
- Select **Windows** → **UV Texture Editor**.

Doing so will show you the UVs of the beast model.

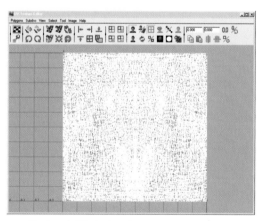

The beast's UVs don't make much sense at this time

3 Project UVs

- With the beast geometry still selected, select **Polygon UVs** → **Planar Mapping** → ❒.

- Set Mapping Direction to Z-axis, then click the **Project** button.

Doing so will cause the UVs to be projected as if you were looking at the beast from the front.

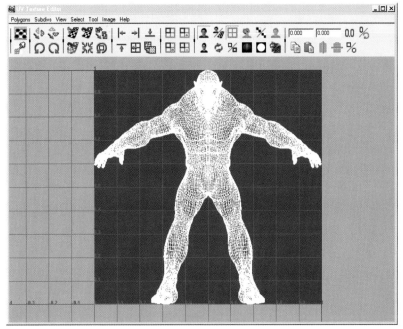

Z-axis projected UVs

4 Assign a checker to the geometry

In order to better see what you are doing on the beast as you unfold the UVs, it is recommended to use a repetitive pattern as the color of the geometry's material.

- **Assign** a new **Lambert** shader to the beast's geometry.

- **Map** a **checker** in the **Color** channel of the new *lambert*.

n **Set** the checker's *place2dTexture*'s Repeat UV to **20** and **20**.

- **Change** the lambert's Texture Resolution from the Hardware Texturing section to Highest (256x256).

5 Save your work

Cut the UVs

In order for the UVs to be properly unfolded, you must first cut the UVs into UV shells, which will define the different parts of the body to be textured. UV shells should be cut and unfolded so that they can lie flat without overlapping, much like a cloth pattern is laid prior to sewing.

The location of the UV cuts requires some planning to obtain the best unfolded result. The better the UV cuts, the better the correlation between the original polygons and their corresponding UV shell. In addition, you should anticipate that the polygon edge cuts will result in texture mismatches along those edges and plan their locations on the model accordingly so they are less visible. For instance, you should cut UVs under the arms or on the back of the legs of a character.

The checker texture assigned to the beast

1   Display the UV borders

- Select **Display** → **Custom Polygon Display** → ❑.

- In the option window, turn **On** the **Highlight Texture Borders** checkbox.

This option will display the UV borders with a thicker line so that they can be easily distinguished.

2   Cut the arm UVs

- Select an edge that is part of an edge ring going around the shoulder at the base of the deltoid.

- Select **Edit Polygons** → **Selection** → **Select Contiguous Edges** or hold **Ctrl** and select **RMB** → **Edge Loop Utilities** → **To Edge Loop**.

This should select a contiguous edge ring around the shoulder.

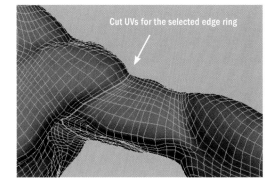

Cut UVs for the selected edge ring

- Select **Polygon UVs** → **Cut UVs**.

You should now see a thicker line where the cut was made.

- Repeat the previous steps in order to cut around the wrist.

- Cut the UVs along the arm starting under the armpit and going under the wrist.

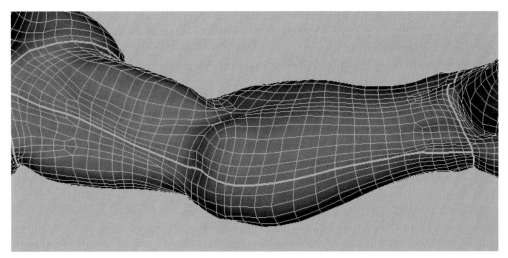

The arm's UVs properly cut

3 Arm UV shell

- In the UV Texture Editor with the geometry selected, **RMB-click** and select **UV**.

- Select a single UV that is part of the arm that you just cut.

- Select **Select** → **Select Shell**.

Doing so will automatically select the UV shell you just created by cutting at the shoulder and wrist.

- Move the UV shell to another location to be able to work on it without overlapping the rest of the beast.

Tip: *You can hide the texture image by selecting Image → Display Image.*

4 Unfold the arm

The **Unfold** command attempts to lay flat a UV shell in order to reduce texture distortion and avoid overlapping UVs. The following will show you the basic usage of this functionality.

- With the arm's UVs still selected, select **Polygons** → **Unfold UVs**.

- Check out the checker pattern on the arm in the Perspective view.

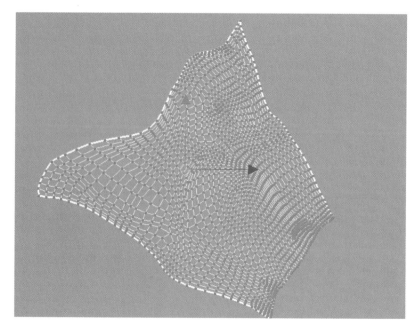

The unfolded UV shell

5 Improve unfolding

The result of the default unfolding is actually quite good, but it could be better.

- Select and move the UVs at the corners of the UV shell and place them to form a rectangle.

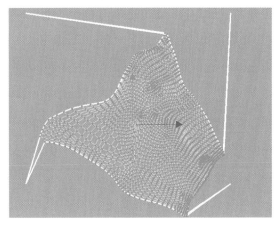

Place the corner UVs to form a rectangle

Tip: Use the **x** hotkey to snap the UVs to the grid.

- Select the entire arm UV shell, then deselect the four corner UVs.

- Select **Polygons** → **Unfold UVs**.

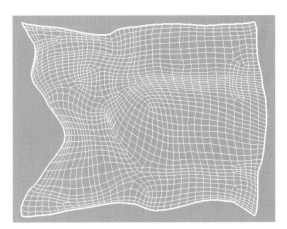

Better arm UV shell unfolding

*The **Unfold** command will affect only the selected UVs. You can unfold this shell to a perfect rectangle by snapping the border UVs to the grid and then selecting all the inner UVs to unfold again.*

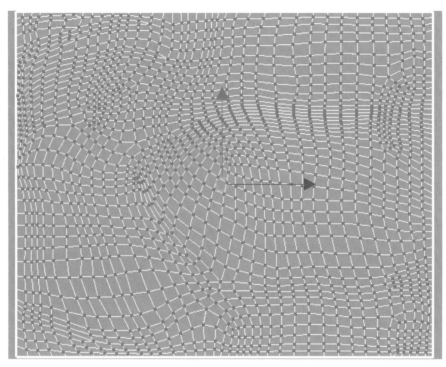

Rectangle UV shell

6 Save your work

- This scene is saved as *05-texture_02.ma* in the support files.

7 Continue unfolding

At this point, you should be able to cut the UVs of the model into UV shells and unfold them to suit your needs.

Tip: *Use the Select Shell Border to decrease the selection of the border UVs.*

> **Note:** *This is a typical workflow and not necessarily what you want to do with all the UV shells of your model.*

Texturing the model

Now that you have a properly unfolded model, you are ready to paint the texture maps. There are several ways of doing this, such as exporting the model in a 3D painting software, but perhaps one of the simplest ways of texturing the beast is in a paint program such as Adobe® Photoshop® .

In order to know how to paint the model and where the details of the geometry are in a paint program, you need to export a UV snapshot, which can be used as a reference to paint on.

1   Export a UV snapshot

- With the beast geometry still selected and visible in the UV Editor, select
  Polygons → **UV Snapshot...**

- In the option window, **browse** for your current project's *sourceimage* directory.

- Set the following:

  Size X and **Y** to **512**;

  Image Format to **TIFF**.

> **Note:** *Depending on where you placed your UV shells, you might want to set a custom* **UV Range.**

- **Click the OK button.**

  An image file is now written to disk, allowing you to paint on it and then use the resulting image as a texture.

2   Using a PSD (Adobe® Photoshop) texture

As an alternative to the UV snapshot, you can use Adobe® Photoshop® (PSD) file textures.

- Press **F5** to change to the **Rendering** menu set.

- Select the geometry that you wish to texture, then select **Texturing** → **Create PSD Network**.

An option window will be displayed.

- In the **Attribute** section, select the different channels that you wish to be accessible for painting and click on the **>** button.

- Click the **Create** button.

A PSD file is now written to disk, allowing you to paint on the different chosen channels and include a UV snapshot.

3   Paint the texture

Open the file created in the previous steps and start painting the model's textures.

4   Textures back in Maya

Once you are done painting the textures, import them back into Maya and see the result on the 3D model. The following image shows the beast's head displacement texture. Open the scene file *05-texture_03.ma* to check out its UVs and texture.

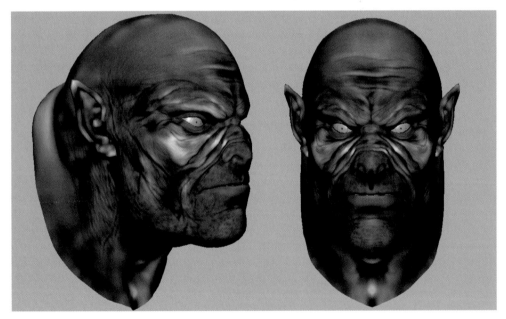

The head's displacement texture

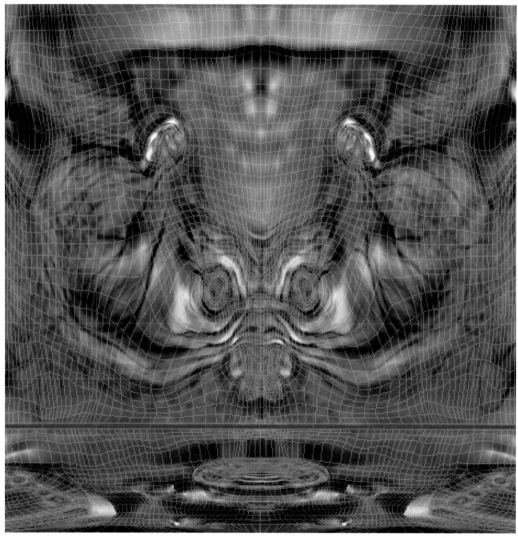

The head's UV shell

Conclusion

In this lesson, you learned a basic workflow to unfold and texture a polygonal model. You have now completed a hyper-real beast model, which will be taken a step further in the next project where you will rig the beast in order to get it ready for animation action.

Rigging
Project Two

In Project Two, you are going to learn techniques and tricks for rigging the beast. The methods discussed in this project can be found within default Maya software and can be applied to any setup needs that you may have. In addition, you will also cover custom MEL tools to enhance your character setup workflow. The concepts explored within this project are intended to be used as ideas that can be applied to any rigging technique or production-ready character.

Lesson 06 *Preparation*

In this lesson, you will be asked to think about what you want to achieve with your character. Taking some time to prepare your work is an essential step in order to minimize time-consuming problems and issues that could arise once a character rig is thoroughly tested in a production pipeline. Doing so will hopefully prevent you and your character from breaking down under the inevitable pressure of deadlines.

In this lesson you will learn the following:

- Definition of character rigging;

- How to prepare yourself;

- How to prepare the character.

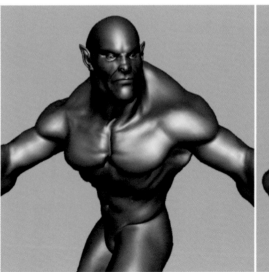

Beast poses

Definition of character rigging

Before you can animate, you need to have a rig built for your creature. Many terms are used for the process of character rigging; you may hear it called set-up, rigging, or puppeting, to name a few.

Rigging is, by far, the most confusing and typically misunderstood procedure in the 3D pipeline process. It can be the most challenging, yet you may find it to be the most rewarding as well. As a rigger, you will most likely find that you are the one everyone relies on to solve problems, create workflows, design and make tools, and simply make everything work.

You have to be continually conscious of making your rig too complex and ultimately unanimatable by you or your animators. It is very easy to fall into the *"Wow! Wouldn't that be cool!"* trap. In the end, the best solution almost always ends up being the simplest one: nothing automated, things easily found in the hierarchy, and very animator-friendly.

Please note that there is not a unique or singular way to make a rig. The ways are countless and each different technique has multiple benefits and downfalls. It is your job to figure out which techniques work best for you and the project at hand.

Prepare yourself

Every creature is unique, as are the needs of each of the animators. For each creature you should always ask yourself certain questions:

- What does the creature physically resemble?

- What does the creature need to do in terms of movements throughout the production?

- Are there special rigs that need to be provided for a few specific shots? If so, in what way do they need to be special?

- Who is animating the creature and what do these artists like in their rigs?

Once you have answered these questions, you need to decide what is most important for the creature. Is it the need of an animator or the need of the show? It is up to you (with input from your lead animator), to make that kind of decision and then to make the rig as easily animatable as possible for the masses using it.

One thing you will always end up doing is looking at real anatomy and wondering how things work and why they move the way they do. To create a successful creature rig, it is essential to understand what is happening underneath the skin of living things. Fill your creature reference arsenal with anatomy books in an effort to gather as much information as possible.

Prepare the character

Before you sit down at the computer, it is recommended to work things out on paper first. Take some Orthographic drawings or screen grabs of the model, print them out, and draw rigging ideas on them. Draw muscle groupings and skeleton locations, take notes, etc. Show the drawings to your coworkers and get their input. Make yourself as familiar with the creature as possible. It will save you time in the long run if you work out a number of issues on paper.

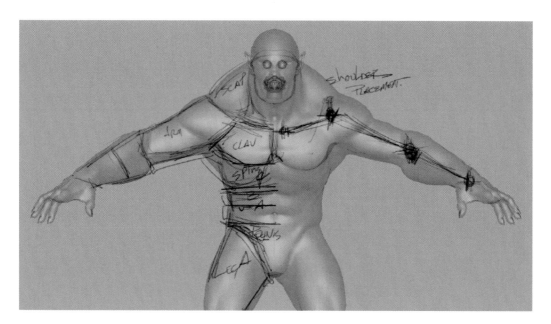

Quick paper drawings serve as guidelines while working on the computer

The last thing you want to do before you start rigging the creature is check the model for anomalies or issues that may hinder your workflow later.

A major thing to look for is if there are any holes or seams in the character model. Holes and seams may be needed for various creatures, but when it comes to weighting they can bring up difficulties. If a hole or seam is needed for the particular creature, the best bet would be to have two versions of the model, one model that is completely *water tight* and continuous, and one that is broken up or seamed. This way you can first bind the seamless creature and paint weights without too much of a hassle, then copy those same weights to the broken up model. This should save you some headaches down the road.

Another thing to watch for is the flow of edge rings or isoparms of the model. To do so, turn **On** the **Wireframe on Shaded** display mode and just look at the model's topology. Look to see if the flow of lines follow major muscle groups, if the definition of the creature is correctly displayed within and if the flow allows for good deformation in the end. This may not be very easy to see in the beginning, but with time and experience you will be able to simply look at a model and see which parts of it will deform well or not.

Be picky with the model's naming convention. You do not want the names of anything to change halfway through the rigging process. This could be another major headache avoided down the road if looked at and dealt with at the beginning. Make sure that the names of all geometry parts follow your standard naming convention.

Most of these issues were already addressed in the first project of this book, so you should not have to make many changes, but it is a good idea to keep all these notes in mind prior to rigging.

Conclusion

Now that you have had a good look at the character and asked yourself questions about its needs, you should envision where you want to go with the character. Doing so sets a good tone for the entire project.

Since learning is done through doing, the next lesson will teach you how to use joint chains, which are the basis of any character rig.

Lesson 07 *Skeleton*

In this lesson, you will learn the rudiments of basic joint creation. Doing so will allow you to create strong rigs with constant orientations, transformations, and naming. You will also use automated tools and MEL scripts in order to speed up the different tasks shown here.

In this lesson you will learn the following:

- Joint chain definition and rules;

- Naming convention;

- Joint's local rotation axis;

- Basic joint creation rules;

- Mirroring joint chains;

- Joint's rotation order;

- How to create joint chains;

- Using automation scripts;

- Broken hierarchies.

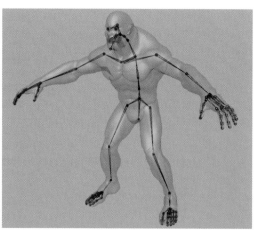

The complete beast skeleton

Joint chain definition

Most deformations of a character will be based on joints. Skeletal joints layout the placement of pivots of the creature's skeletal articulations.

A joint chain is any group of joints and their bones connected in a series. The joints are connected linearly; you could draw a line through a joint chain's series of joints and their bones without having to retrace your path. A given joint chain begins at the highest joint in the joint chain's hierarchy. This joint is the chain's *parent joint*.

Joint chains can also be thought of as sets of joints that build up specific parts of a creature. The spine, the arms, the hands and the fingers are all examples of joint chains.

Naming convention

Every studio, if not production, will have its own set of naming conventions. It is extremely important to have a general set of rules everyone follows so that anyone can jump into any rig and find what they are looking for by simply glancing at the names.

Following is an example of the naming convention used in this book:

armJALf_1

- The name starts with a description of the node group or joint chain.

- It is followed by the type of node it is, such as **J** for a joint, **G** for a group node, etc.

- It then has a node letter. For a joint chain, each child joint in a single chain has its own letter. The last joint will be called **JEnd**.

- Then comes the side of the chain, such as **Lf**, **Rt** or blank for neither.

- Finally, **_1** is at the end of every node, which allows you to visually ensure there is only one node with such a name, since Maya software usually adds or increments the number at the end of a name when it is duplicated.

⊟ armJALf_1
⊟   armJBlf_1
⊟   armJClf_1
        armJEndlf_1

Standardized naming convention

> **Note:** Of course, this is just an example of one naming convention. Feel free to implement anything that suits you and your studio's needs, but be aware that the scripts used for automation in this book are based on this naming convention.

Local rotation axis

Every joint has a *Local Rotation Axis* that defines how the joint will react to transformations.

When you create several joints in a row, the joint orientations can automatically be set to point down to the first child joint. A joint's orientation is defined by its local rotation axis, which is, by default, pointing the **X-axis** toward its first child joint.

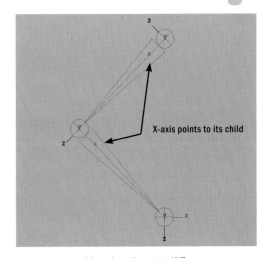

X-axis points to its child

Joint orientation set to XYZ

> **Note:** Local rotation axes are aligned according to the left-hand rule, which are the three axes defined by your index (**X-axis**), thumb (**Y-axis**) and middle (**Z-axis**) fingers when pointing out at right angles. For example, if you select an orientation of **XYZ**, the positive X-axis points into the joint's bone and towards the joint's first child joint, the Y-axis points at right angles to the X and Z-axes and the Z-axis points sideways from the joint and its bone.

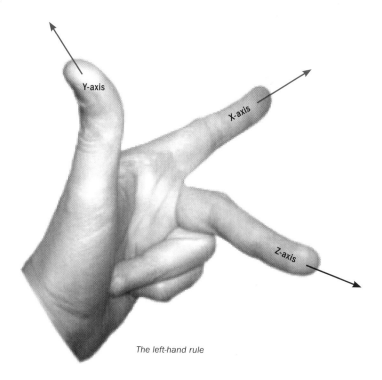

The left-hand rule

The local rotation axes are often used to define the rotation axes correctly to achieve good bending, but they will also determine the translation values of a joint to its parent.

A recommended technique is to ultimately have all joints in your skeleton at their default pose. This would mean having **0.0** values in their **Translate Y**, **Translate Z** and **Rotate** attributes and **1.0** as their **Scale**, leaving only the **Translate X** attribute with a value, which is the length of the joint down the chain.

To place a child joint in the correct orientation and location, you should only use the local **Translate X** attribute. All the other attributes will then stay with their default values. Respecting this rule will make it very easy to reset your skeleton to its default position.

> **Note:** *Obviously, this rule can be broken while placing the joints in the creature's geometry, but their attributes will eventually need to be reset to follow the convention.*

Basic joint creation rules

Following are the general rules for a basic joint chain:

- Only the parent joint can have translation values in X, Y and Z. Every other joint in the chain should only have a **Translate X** value.

- All joints in the chain should have **0.0** values in all the **Rotation** attributes. Joint rotations are only used to initially rotate the joint into position.

- All joints in the chain should have values of **1.0** in **Scale**.

- Joint orientation should be adjusted so the joint can rotate around the positive **Z-axis** in a forward motion in most instances. This will ease the reading of animation curves in the Graph Editor and provide an idea of what the animation is without even looking in the camera views.

- The end joint of the chain should have **0.0** values in the **Joint Orient XYZ** as well.

Mirroring chains

When working on a symmetrical rig, the left and right sides of the creature should be mirrored so that the animator can grab the corresponding left and right joints and rotate them in one axis to be a perfect mirror of each other.

The following shows how to mirror a complete side of the creature's joint chains.

1   Scene file

- Open the scene file *07-mirror_01.ma*.

This scene contains half of the creature's skeleton ready for you to mirror to the other side.

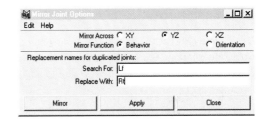

The mirror joint options

2   Mirror the joint chains

- Select the clavicle joint named *clavJALf_1*.

- Select **Skeleton → Mirror Joint → ❑**.

- In the tool options, set **Mirror Across** to **YZ** and set **Mirror Function** to **Behavior**.

- In the **Replacement names for duplicate joints** section, set **Search For** to *Lf* and

  Replace With to *Rt*.

Doing so will let the tool know how to automatically rename the new joints according to your naming convention.

- Click on the **Mirror** button.

- **Execute** the tool again to mirror the legs.

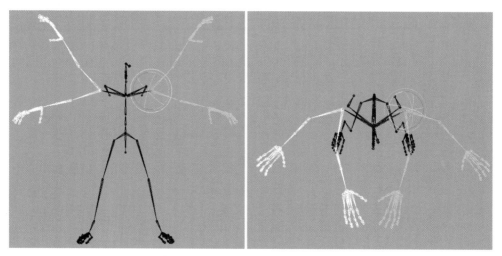

The behavior of the joints is perfectly mirrored

3   Test the joints' behavior

- Select both shoulder joints and rotate them to see the effect of the **Mirror Joint Tool**.

> **Note:**   *Mirroring joint chains basically duplicates the joints, mirrors their positions and flips over their local rotation axes.*

Joint rotation order

The *joint's rotation order* is just as important as the joint's local rotation axis. It determines in which order the X, Y and Z rotations are applied onto the object.

The best way of understanding the rotation order is to use the **Rotate Tool** with the **Gimbal** option turned **On**. Using the manipulator that way, you will see that X rotations do not affect the Y and Z values, Y rotations affect the X values but not the Z values, and Z rotations affect both the Y and X values. Mathematically, this means that Maya calculates the object's matrix Z rotation first, then the Y rotation and then the X rotation.

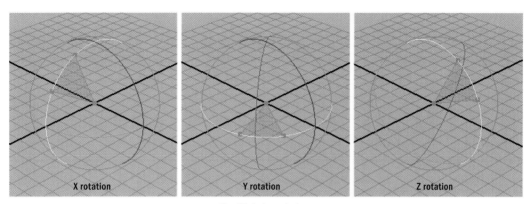

X rotation   Y rotation   Z rotation

The Gimbal manipulator

The default **Rotation Order** is **XYZ**, which means that the rotations are applied in opposite order. This may seem complex at first, but understanding the core of rotation calculation will eventually help you figure out and prevent any rotation problems you may experience in your production, such as *Gimbal Lock*.

> **Note:** *Gimbal Lock is caused when the second axis in the rotation order is rotated in such a way that the two other rotation axes get on top of each other. When this happens, rotating any of the two other axes will result in the same rotational effect on the object. Thus, changing the rotation order in consideration of your character's range of movement can make Gimbal Lock less probable.*

After creation of the joint chain, you can set it to any order you want through the Attribute Editor. In general, using **XYZ** is relatively safe to start with. But, don't limit yourself to just using this rotation order; switch them as needed and try them out. However, make sure you switch them before any animation is done.

> **Note:** *While setting up a different rotation order is uncomplicated for the average animator, changing it after animation is done will affect the animation. Fixing such an issue can be done, but is not a simple task.*

Joint chain creation

Before you can learn the automated way of joint creation, you need to understand how to layout joints the hard way. Based on the rules explained in the previous section, only the parent joint can have values in the Y and Z translation attributes. Also, you have to have the joint's local rotation axes lined up correctly with your model's bending orientations.

1   Scene file

- Open the scene file *07-beastModel_01.ma.*

This scene contains the finalized beast from the first project.

2   Creating a simple joint chain

- Select **Skeleton** → **Joint Tool**.

- In the *front* view, create three joints holding down **Shift** as in the following image, then press **Enter** to exit the tool.

Holding down **Shift** *will create the joint chain in a perfect straight line.*

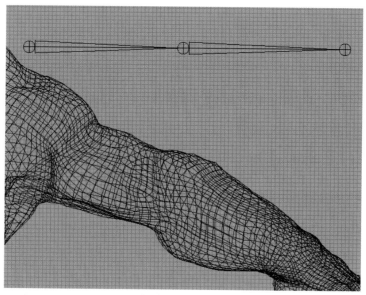

The straight arm joint chain

> **Tip:**   *If the joint display size is too small, increase the* **Display** → **Joint Size.**

3 Place the joint chain

- From the *Perspective* view, place the **parent joint** at the appropriate XYZ location in the shoulder of the model.

4 Rotate the joint

- With the parent joint still selected, open the Attribute Editor.

- In the **Joint** section, use the **Joint Orient** attributes to rotate the joint in the upper arm, making sure to place the elbow joint at the correct location.

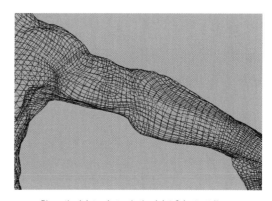

*Place the joint using only the **Joint Orient** attributes*

Tip: Hold down **Ctrl** and **click+drag** in an attribute field to change the attribute value interactively. The **LMB** will change the value by increments of **0.01**, the **MMB** by increments of **0.1** and the **RMB** by increments of **1.0**.

5 Elbow joint

- Press the **Down** arrow key to select the elbow joint.

- **Double-click** on the **Move Tool** in the toolbox.

The options for the tool will be displayed.

- Set the **Move** option to **Local**.

- **Translate** the elbow joint to its appropriate location using only the **X-axis**.

- Use the **Joint Orient** attributes to set the joint's orientation and align the wrist.

6 Wrist joint

- **Translate** the wrist joint on its **X-axis** to place it correctly in the geometry.

- Since this is an end joint, make sure to set all of its **Joint Orient** attributes to **0.0**.

Note: This example shows you what happens with the joints when you place them and then reset their attributes, using such tools as Freeze Transformations. Rotation values go in the Joint Orient, allowing the Rotate attributes to be zeroed out.

Scripts for automation

Now that you have learned the true workings of how to create the ideal joint chain, here is a much more visual approach. The *templateSkeletonLE.mel* script should help you quickly edit the names and orientations of joint chains with just a few mouse clicks. This automated tool will make the creation of your joint chains or any creature rig much easier.

1   Source

Source the templateSkeletonLE.mel script in Maya software by doing one of the following:

- **Drag+drop** the script from the support_files directory.

Or

- Select **File** → **Source** from the Script Editor and **browse** for the script.

Or

- **Copy** the content of the script to one of your shelves.

2   Execute the script

- To execute the script, type the following in the Command Line:

    templateSkeletonLE

An option window for the tool will be displayed.

3   Try the script

- Click on the **Joint** button in the option window.

This is just a shortcut to the Maya software Joint Tool.

- **Create** a simple joint chain for the sake of this example and press **Enter**.

- With the parent joint selected, click the **Template** button.

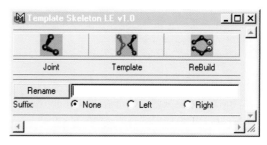

The templateSkeletonLE.mel option window

Doing so will create a hierarchy of specific nodes allowing the script to work. You will see in the viewport that there is one locator for each joint except for the last one in the chain. There were also attributes added to the joints that will allow you to orient the local rotation axis.

Note: *To edit the size of the visual locators of the joint chain, change the Rot Gui Scale attribute on the top node of the tool's hierarchy.*

4   Tweak the joint chain

- Change the position of the joint chain using the **Move**, **Rotate** or **Scale Tool**, like you would normally do to place it within a character's geometry.

- Using the new **Rot Gui** attribute on the joints, adjust the rotation direction of the joint so that the locator is in the direction you want the *positive Z-axis rotation* to be.

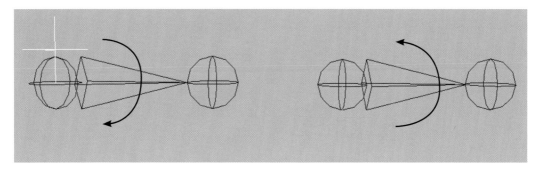

The position of the locator defines the Z position rotation

5   Rebuild the joint chain

- Once your editing of the joint chain is complete, select the top node of the tool's hierarchy, in this case *templateSkeletonN_1*.

- Click on the **Rebuild** button in the option window.

After rebuilding the templateSkeleton hierarchy, your joint chain will have proper attribute values and the correct local rotation axis.

6   Rename the joint chain

Now that you have a newly created joint chain, remember that you have to name it correctly with your set naming convention. The *templateSkeletonLE.mel* tool has a naming feature built into it to quickly name the entire chain.

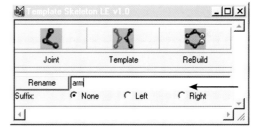

The Rename text field

- Select the joint that you want to be the top of the chain.

Typically, this would be the parent joint of the hierarchy, but the tool doesn't limit you to this.

- In the **Rename** text field of the option window, enter the name of the joint chain, for instance, *arm*, *spine*, *hand*, etc.

- Set the **Suffix** option to be the appropriate suffix of your joint chain.

- Click on the **Rename** button.

The tool will automatically rename the joint chain with the appropriate naming convention.

> **Note:** *If you require a different naming convention, you will need to bring changes to the templateSkeletonLE.mel script.*

- **Repeat** as needed.

*One thing to notice with the renaming feature is that the tool will automatically set the **Joint Labelling** attributes of the joint, which will ease the workload if you wish to use the animation retargeting feature of Maya software.*

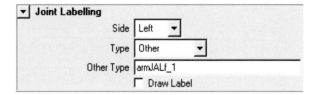

The Joint Labelling attributes set to be used with animation retargeting

Broken hierarchies

A technique for giving the animator an extreme amount of control with the character is the *broken hierarchy technique*. This technique has each specific joint chain of the character separated, and then connected via point and animatable orient constraints that give each section the ability to follow or have independent motion from its parent. It may start off as a confusing idea, but once you get the hang of it and try some animations with it, you will find the advantages pretty quickly.

1   Scene file

- Open the scene file *07-brokenHierarchies.ma*.

This scene file contains a simplified version of the beast's skeleton with IKs, built on the broken hierarchy technique.

2   See what it does

- Through the Outliner, select the *bodyJ_1* joint.

- **Rotate** the joint on the **Z-axis** and watch the skeleton react.

Notice that the hands and feet are not planted in orientation when you rotate the body.

- Select the *configN_1* node.

*Notice all the Ori attributes in the Channel Box. These attributes control the orientation of each joint chain. They go from **0.0** to **1.0**, where **0.0** orients the chain as the world and **1.0** orients the chain according to the parent joint chain.*

- Set all of the **Ori** attributes of the *configN_1* node to **0.0**.

- Select the *bodyJ_1* joint and **rotate** the joint on the **Z-axis** again.

Notice that all the different joint chains now have world orientations.

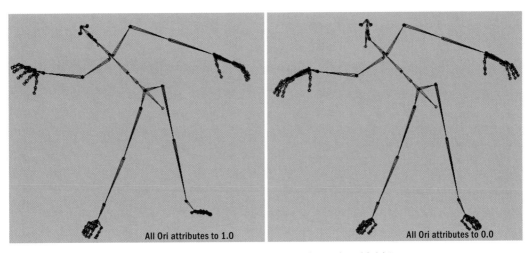

Orientation differences with the same rotation on the pelvis joint

Note: *You can animate all the different Ori attributes independently throughout your animations.*

Broken hierarchy setup

In the following section, you will redo a portion of the broken hierarchy setup from the last example scene.

The trick used in the broken hierarchy setup is that before applying the individual point and orient constraints to the top of each joint chain, you want to add a duplicated joint right on top of the parent joint. This new joint will receive the constraints so that you can still cleanly animate the first joint of the chain. The following shows how to set-up this type of setup.

1   Scene file

- Create a **new** scene file.

- From the *top* view, **create** two separate joint chains to form an arm and a hand as follows:

- **Rename** the joints appropriately following the naming convention using the *templateSkeletonLE* tool.

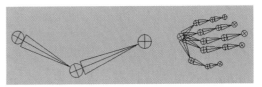

Two distinct joint chains

- Select the hand's parent joint and snap it to the end joint of the arm chain using the **v** hotkey.

2   Create the duplicate parent joint

- Select the hand parent joint chain.

- **Duplicate** the hand chain.

- Through the Outliner, **delete** all children of this duplicated chain.

Doing so will leave you with a duplicated joint at the exact location and values of the original joint chain.

- **Rename** the duplicated joint to *handJCon_1*.

- **Parent** the original hand joint to the *handJCon_1* joint.

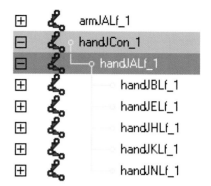

The new hierarchy

3   Save your work

- Save the scene as *07-brokenHierarchies_02.ma*.

Constraining manually

At this point, it is best to continue learning the hard way of doing things before trying the easy automated way. The following will show you how the constraining was done in the character example shown earlier. It consists of creating two copies of the JCon joint, one for world orientation and the other for its parent, and then constraining the JCon with an orient constraint that will be driven with Set Driven Keys.

1   Scene file

- Open the scene file *07-brokenHierarchies_02.ma* from the last example.

2   Point constrain the hand chain

- **Duplicate** the hand's *handJCon_1*.

- **Delete** all the children of the new joint chain, then rename the joint to *handJOri_1*.

- **Parent** this new joint underneath the *armJEnd_1* joint of the arm chain.

You now have four joints on top of each other at the wrist location. Each of these joints will have their own purpose in the setup.

- Select the *armJEnd_1* joint, then **Ctrl-select** the *handJCon_1* in the Outliner.

- Select Constrain → **Point**.

The handJCon_1 joint will now follow in position the end joint of the arm.

3   Orient constrain the hand chain

- With nothing selected, press **Ctrl+g** to create an empty group.

- **Rename** the group to *handOriGrpN_1*.

- **Parent** this group to the *handJCon_1*, **zero** all of its **Rotate** attributes, then press **Shift+p** to **unparent** the group.

This is a simple little trick to set the group's rotation to be the same as the handJCon_1.

- Select the *handOriGrpN_1*, then **Ctrl-select** the *handJOri_1* **and** *handJCon_1* in the Outliner.

- Select **Constrain** → **Orient**.

This will constrain the handJCon_1 joint to both the handOriGrpN_1 and handJOri_1. You can then set the orientation to follow either the world orientation or the arm's orientation.

4 Create a control attribute

In order to easily control the constraint created in the previous step, you will need to set-up a node with a custom attribute that will drive the orientation constraint's attributes.

- **Create** an empty group and **rename** it to *configN_1*.

- Select **Modify** → **Add Attribute** and set the following:

  Attribute Name to *handOri*;

  Data Type to **Float**;

  Minimum to **0**;

  Maximum to **1**.

- Click on the **OK** button.

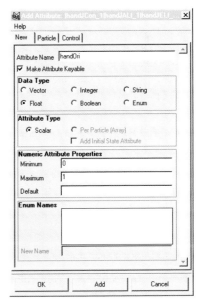

The Add Attribute window

5 Set Driven Keys

- Select **Animate** → **Set Driven Key** → **Set** → ☐.

- **Load** the *configN_1* node as the **Driver** and highlight the *handOri* attribute.

- **Load** the hand's orient constraint as the **Driven** and highlight the *handOriGrpN_1W0* and *handJOri_1W1* attributes.

- **Set** the first driven key as follows:

  handOri set to **0**;
  handOriGrpN_1W0 set to **1**;
  handJOri_1W1 set to **0**.

- **Set** the second driven key as follows:

  handOri set to **1**;
  handOriGrpN_1W0 set to **0**;
  handJOri_1W1 set to **1**.

6   Test the setup

- When rotating the arm's parent joint with the *configN_1* node's *handOri* attribute set to **0**, the hand should follow the world's orientation.

This way, you can animate the hand's rotation separately from the rest of the arm chain.

- When rotating the arm's parent joint with the *configN_1* node's *handOri* attribute set to **1**, the hand should follow the orientation of the *armJEnd_1* joint.

This way, you can animate the hand just like if the hand was part of the arm's hierarchy.

- Try to animate the *configN_1* node's *handOri* attribute to see its effect on animation.

- Try to add an IK handle on the arm chain to see the setup react with inverse kinematics.

Constraining automatically

Now that you know how to create animatable, independent orientation setups, you will use a tool to help set this all simply with a few options and clicks.

1   Scene file

- Open the scene file *07-brokenHierarchies_02.ma* before you create the constraints manually.

2   Source the script

- **Source** the *HRRoriConstraint.mel* script in Maya.

- **Execute** `HRRoriConsWin` to display the tool's options.

- Select the *handJCon_1* joint and then **Ctrl-select** the *armJEnd_1* joint in the Outliner.

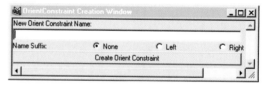

- In the tool window, enter a proper name in the **New Orient Constraint Name** field, such as *hand*, and then specify the proper **Name Suffix**.

The Orient Constraint Tool window

- Click the **Create Orient Constraint** button.

The tool will add the point and orient constraints as needed, create all the needed controls and set all the proper attributes.

3   Test the setup

> **Note:**   *If the configN_1 or orientsN_1 nodes already exist, the tool will append the required nodes or attributes to them.*

Beast Skeleton

As stated in the previous lesson, the best rigs are usually the simplest and cleanest rigs. You want enough control for the animators to get just about everything they need, but you don't want to over-complicate anything. You need the animators to have the creature look good. If they fight with the rig or the playback speed, most likely the animation will tend to look very unnatural or strange in the end.

Luckily, the beast example character is a symmetrical model, meaning that you will only have to rig half of it and mirror the other half, saving time, even in weighting!

When lying out the joints for the beast, be mindful of the topology flow and make sure the joint orientations go along with the model, not the world axis. Another thing to keep in mind when adjusting the orientations is that you want all the positive Z rotations of the joints to go forward for the creature.

> **Note:** The rig setup built here is very generic and will work nicely for the sake of this example. You may have specific needs that this rig does not address.

The spine, neck, head and pelvis

The basis of all motion in a character generally stems from the spine and pelvis connection. As such, you will start by creating the spine. For a humanoid creature, most flexibility comes from the lumbar section of the spine underneath the rib cage. This means that there will be less flexibility in the rib cage.

The best natural animation for a spine really comes from a simple FK spine. It gives the animators the exact control they need to get the correct motion and poses for a shot.

1   Scene file

- Open the scene file *07-beastModel_01.ma*.

  This scene contains only the original beast geometry.

2   Draw the joints

- From the *side* view, **draw** the first spine joint and place it at the connection point from the pelvis to the spine.

- **Draw** three other joints as follows:

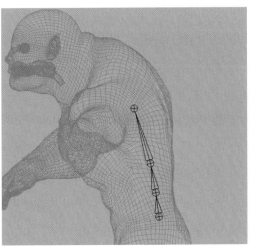

Spine joint chain

The first two joints are evenly spaced and closer together because most of the rotation will come from this area. The last two joints are longer because there will be few deformations in the rib cage area.

- Continue drawing two joints for the neck spaced evenly, and then place another joint at the base of the head.

- Complete this chain by drawing a last joint at the top of the head and hitting **Enter**.

This last joint is only for visual reference purposes to see where the head is and determine when the animator animates with the geometry hidden.

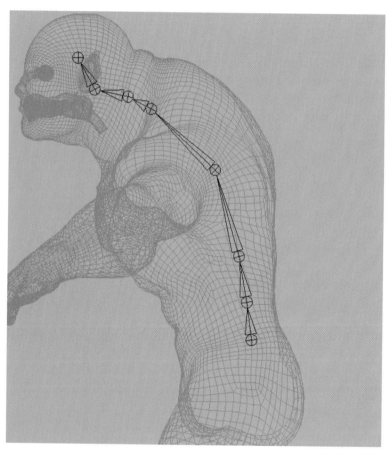

Neck and head joint chains

- **Draw** two other joints for the pelvis and press **Enter**. Snap the first joint on the first spine joint and then the other one on the lower tip of the pelvis in the crotch area.

- **Create** one last joint in space and then **snap** it to the first spine joint.

3   Rename and orient the joints

- Rename this last joint to *bodyJ_1*.

This will be the connection of spine and pelvis at the root joint.

- **Parent** both the *spine* and *pelvis* joint chains to the *bodyJ_1* joint.

Having the bodyJ_1 joint as the parent joint, or root, of the chain will allow both the pelvis and the spine to rotate independently from each other.

- Use the *templateSkeletonLE.mel* script to **orient** and **rename** the different joint chains.

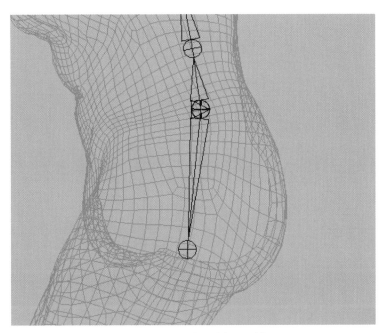

The pelvis joint chain and the root joint

For orientation, remember that you should set positive Z rotations of the joints moving forward. Meaning, if you were to grab all the joints in the spine, neck and head and rotate them in positive Z simultaneously, they would all rotate towards the front of the character. The pelvis is actually an exception to this rule and should rotate backwards.

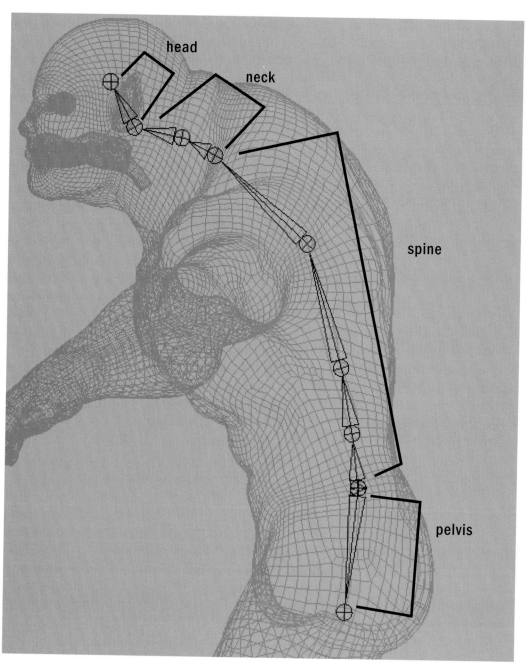

Prefixes and orientations for the different portions of the chains

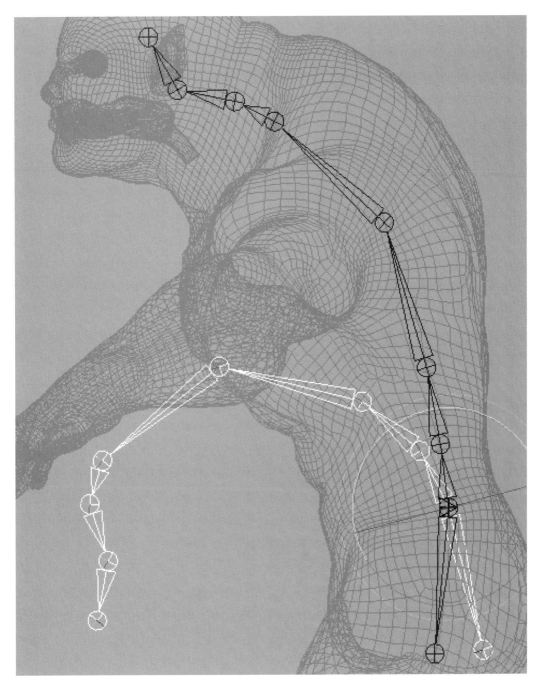

The new joints with positive Z rotations

4   **Save your work**

The leg and foot

The hip placement for humanoid legs is always extremely crucial for good deformation. As always, look to real anatomy and you will see that the leg connects into the pelvis a bit higher than most people would think. As for the foot, if you don't have toes in the model, for instance, with a shoed character, you can get away with just two bones, one from ankle to ball of the foot, and another one from ball to the tip of the toes. This is not the case for the beast so you will have to rig all of its toes as well. The one other thing to consider is the end of the foot placement joint. This is actually where you would pivot from with a reverse foot setup. When animating, you mainly pivot off the ball of the foot, not the tip of the toes.

5   Draw leg joints

- Still in the *side* view, **draw** joints starting from the hip, to the knee, to the ankle.

- Continue drawing a joint about mid-foot and then complete the chain with a joint at the beginning of the toes on the model.

6   Place the joints

- Take care to check through multiple views to make sure that the joint orientations are lined up with the model.

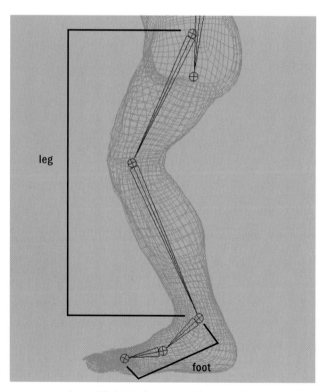

Leg and foot joint placements and name prefixes

- Use *templateSkeleton* to correctly **orient** and **rename** the joints.

Joint orientation for the legs should be positive Z forward and continue into the feet.

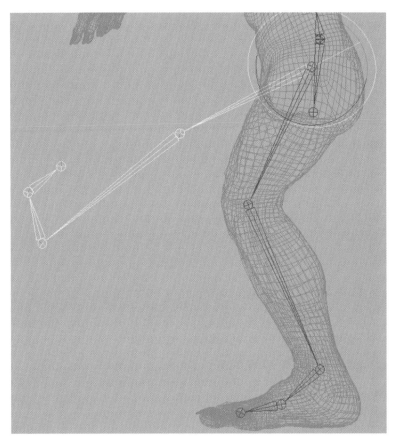

Leg and foot positive Z rotations

The toes

Since the beast has toes, you will have to rig them too. The beast's toes are rather long and an animator may want to curl them to hit the sought after pose.

7 Create the big toe chain

- From the *top* view, draw four joints for the big toe. Start with one at the metatarsals, then another at the beginning of the toe, then one in the middle of the toe and finish the chain with one at the tip of the toe geometry.

Of course, the big toe tends not to bend in the middle, but you never know what an animator may want, and this will come in handy for the rest of the toes because you will duplicate the chain for the other toes and they will require four joints.

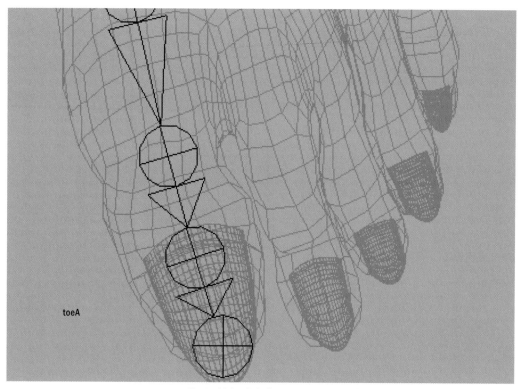

The toeA joint chain from top view

- **Place**, **orient** and **rename** the *toeA* joint chain correctly.

8 Create the other toes

- **Duplicate** the joint chain and move it for the next toe.

Make sure all the joints fit in the toe's topology by looking in different views.

- **Rename** the new chain to *toeB*.

- **Repeat** the previous steps to create the remaining toes.

- **Parent** all the toe chains to the *footJB_1* joint.

9 Save your work

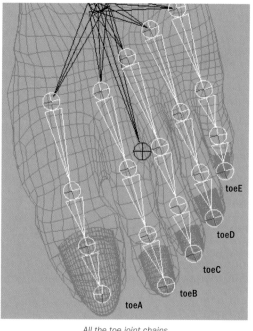

All the toe joint chains

The clavicle, arm and hand

Think of the clavicle as part of the arm and create it as one entity continuing into the hand.

As difficult as hip placement is, the shoulder is much harder. So many things are going on in that region during deformation, and there are a number of influences you need to watch to achieve just one simple pose like moving the arm up or down. Finding the correct shoulder joint placement is very important. To help you do this, you may wish to create a few joints, bind the skin to them, and then test rotations just to see if you have it right.

Then, as if the shoulder is not complicated enough, you have the elbow, hand and fingers. The amount of work necessary for the hand, finger and wrist area is about the same as it takes to do the entire rest of the body.

10 Create the arm

- From the *front* view, **draw** the arm joint chain starting from the clavicle base, extending to the shoulder, the elbow, the wrist, and finally, to the end of the hand, just before the finger geometry.

- **Parent** the joint chain to the *spineJF_1*.

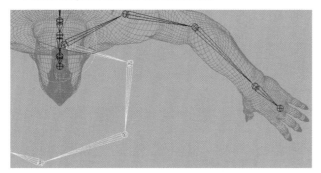

The arm joint chain location and prefixes

- **Place, orient** and **rename** the joints correctly.

The orientation of the joints for the arm should again bend on positive Z toward the front of the character.

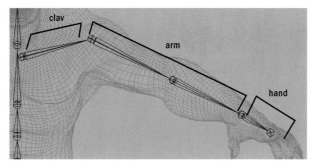

The positive Z rotation of the arm chain

11 Create the index finger

- In the *top* view, **draw** five joints for the index finger, starting at the metacarpal, going to the knuckle, then the two finger joints, and finally one at the tip of the finger.

- **Place** and **orient** the finger chain.

The orientation for the finger should be positive Z when rotating toward the palm of the hand to form a fist. When doing this, you will most likely have to individually adjust each joint with the topology to get the correct curl motion. As always, remember to continually check different camera angles to get the joint locations right.

- **Rename** the chain with the *indFng* prefix.

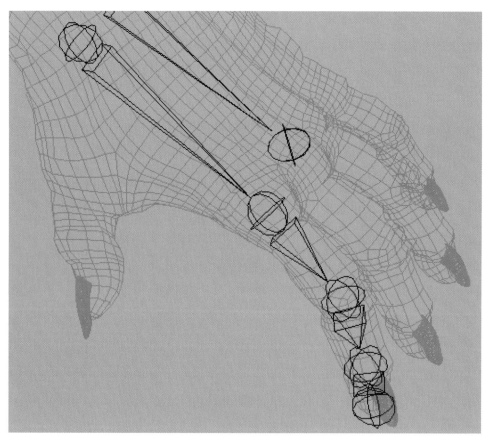

Location of the index finger joints

12 Create the other fingers

- **Duplicate** the index finger to create the other fingers.

- **Move** and **orient** the joints correctly.

- **Rename** the finger chains to *midFng*, *rngFng* and *pnkyFng*.

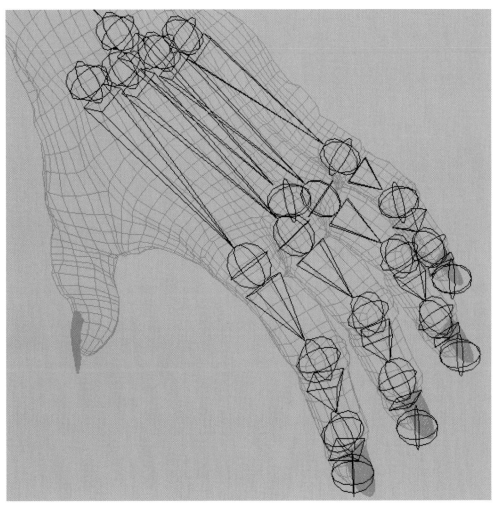

All the finger joint chains

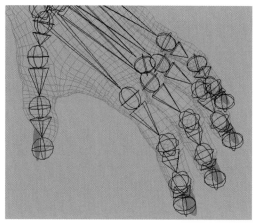

The hand joint chains completed

13 Create the thumb

- **Duplicate** the last four joints of the index chain, then **move** and **orient** the joints correctly for the thumb.

The thumb's position Z rotations should also point toward the palm of the hand to form a fist.

- **Rename** the thumb chain with the *thmb* prefix.

- **Parent** all the finger and thumb chains to *handJA_1*.

14 Save your work

Note: Make sure that you can easily form a fist with a single rotation on all the fingers at the same time.

The jaw

The jaw is one simple bone. Eventually, you will hook this joint into the facial rig system, but for now, you will keep it simple with just an open and close motion.

15 Create the jaw bone

- From the *top* view, **draw** two joints for the jaw, one at the hinge of the jaw, and the other at the tip of the chin geometry.

- **Orient** and **rename** the jaw joints with the *jaw* prefix.

The orientation of the jaw should be a continuation and follow the angles of the head, meaning that positive Z rotation is for opening the jaw wider.

- **Parent** the jaw chain under *headJ_1*.

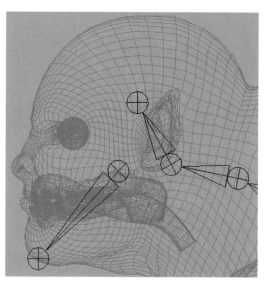

The jaw placement

Note: In the next project, you will be taking the jaw and head setup to the next level.

The eyes

The eyes are just as simple as the jaw, if not simpler since you don't have to guess where to place the joints. The main thing to remember while creating the eyes is that their behavior is not mirrored side to side like everything else will be. For example, if you were to grab both eye controls at the same time and rotate on the Y-axis, you would want them to move in the same direction rather than crossed.

You will have to place two joints for the eye: one in the very center of the spherical eyeball, and another one at the center of the pupil. There are multiple ways to create a joint at the center of an object. Since the beast's eyes are perfectly round NURBS spheres, this will be quite easy.

16 Create the eye joints

- In the *side* view, **create** a single joint.

- **Point constraint** the new joint to the left eyeball sphere.

This is a simple trick to move the joint to the correct location in the eye.

Note: *If the joint does not move, make sure to turn* **Off** *the* **Maintain Offset** *flag in the constraint options.*

- **Delete** the point constraint you just created.

- **Create** another joint and hold down **v** to snap to the central CV of the pupil geometry.

- **Rename** the joint chain with the eye prefix.

- **Keep** the default orientation for the eye joints.

- **Parent** the new joint to the other joint in the center of the eye.

- **Parent** the joint chain to *headJEnd_1*.

17 Create the other eye

Because the model is centered at the origin, you can create the right eye simply by duplicating the chain.

- **Duplicate** the *eyeJLf_1* joint chain.

- Use the same trick as in the previous step to point constraint the joint in the center of the other eye geometry and then delete the constraint.

- **Rename** the joint chain correctly and keep the default orientation of the joints.

Mirroring the joints

Now that you have created all the joint chains needed on one side of the beast, you need to recreate the exact same chains on the opposite side, but with mirrored behavior. Using the **Mirror Joint Tool** to do this will give you exactly what you need with ease. It even renames the joints correctly.

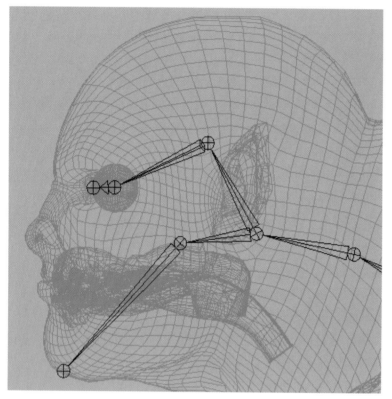

The eye joint chain placement

18 Mirror the joint chains

For each of the joint chains to mirror, do the following:

- Select the parent joint of the joint chain.

- Select **Skeleton** → **Mirror Joint** → ❏ and set the options as follows:

  Mirror Across to **YZ**;
  Behavior to **Mirror Function**;
  Search for *Lf*;
  Replace with *Rt*.

- Click the **Mirror** button.

19 Save your work

- Save your scene as *07-rig_01.ma*.

Conclusion

In this lesson, you learned about several basic skeletal theories, about different conventions used, and about scripts that automate some repetitive tasks.

In the next lesson, you will start rigging the beast's skeleton.

Lesson 08 *Control rig*

In this lesson, you will be creating two distinct rigs. One rig will be used for the bound character and another will be used as the animator-friendly control rig. These two rigs will then be connected together with useful MEL scripts. You will also learn how to structure your hierarchies in order for everyone working with you to easily find what they are looking for.

In this lesson you will learn the following:

- Multiple rig workflow;

- Some more automation with MEL scripts;

- Hierarchy structure convention;

- Semi-automated scapula set-up.

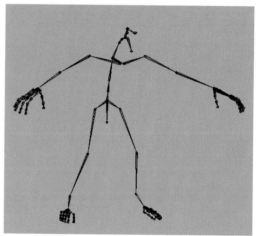

The high resolution rig, the control rig and the skeleton

Multiple rigs

It is smart when creating rigs to use multiple rigs for a single creature. Basically, the idea is to keep the scene as light as possible at all times, and to give you the ability to have different rigs for different needs. The main goal is to have a control rig that is simply a low resolution animation rig with all the necessary controls, and a basic bound rig that is the renderable creature with a simple rig, for instance, a basic motion capture rig without IK. The animator would animate with the control rig, which can be scrubbed in real time in the scene, and then at render time, hook up the bound rig to it so that the control rig drives the bound one via standard point and orient constraints.

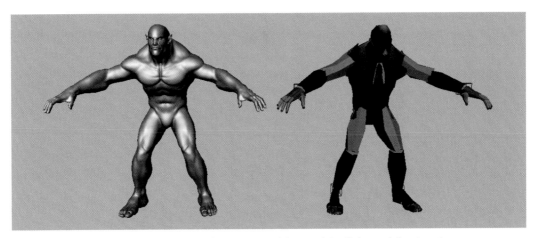

The bound rig with high resolution geometry and the control rig with low resolution geometry

Another advantage to a technique like this is that you can hand off the control rig to the animator as soon as you are done, and then start the weighting process of the bound rig. This way, the animators are not sitting around waiting.

Then, as you make revisions to the bound rig (which is likely to happen since you may be adding blend shapes, new weighting, if not even new model topology, etc.), the animators can just delete the old bound rig and hook up the new one without having to worry about any animation transfer issues.

One more thing that animators enjoy with multi rigs is the ability to add new nodes into their control hierarchies while still being able to hook up and control their bound rigs as needed. This allows them to add numerous nodes to a chain when they run into issues, such as Gimbal Lock, for example.

Before you can hook up the two rigs, you need to add some hidden attributes onto both the control rig and bound rig joints. All of these are message attributes that store the joint's original name (in case the name accidentally changes), and the corresponding joint to look for and hook up to.

Both the control and bound rigs should be saved as separate individual files with the following tasks executed in each of them:

The control rig

You will need to add a control attribute to all of the driver joints for the creature. These are the joints that actually deform the skin or act as controls of the bound file. In other words, these would be every joint in the scene but the *JCon* and the *JOri* nodes. You can do this using an automated MEL script.

The bound rig

On each joint that is controlled by another from the control rig, you will add a hidden message attribute that will let the connection tools find and hook up the joint to its driver. This will be done simply by selecting all the joints in the bound rig character and running another automated MEL script.

Connecting the rigs together

To do this task, you will run another automated MEL script that will look at the two hierarchies and match up the new bound attributes. If the script finds a match it will connect the bound joint to the control via a point and orient constraint. It will also add the bound rig top node into a layer and make a reference for ease of animation. You will then be able to pursue your animation on the control rig as normal and the bound will follow accordingly.

> **Note:** *Not all controls need be in the control rig. For instance, you can decide to have the tongue of the beast only in the bound rig if you wish. Just remember if you do such things, you will need to use animation transfers on those certain parts for updating the puppets.*

The bound rig

You will now implement the multi rig technique with the beast. Each puppet will have hidden attributes that tell automated tools which joint drives what.

Maya software is namespace sensitive, meaning that everything in a scene has to have a unique name, so you will add a prefix to every joint in the bound rig.

> **Note:** *It is possible to have two completely different hierarchies with the same names in each, with only a different name for the top node. You might be able to get away with this, but you would always have to bother using the pipe character [|] in the names and scripts.*

1   **Scene file**

- Open the scene file *07-rig_01.ma*.

   Or

- Continue with your own scene.

2   **Prefix the hierarchy of the bound rig**

- Select the *bodyJ_1* joint.

- Select **Modify** → **Prefix Hierarchy Nam**es and enter *HRR_* as the prefix to use.

   Doing so will prefix the entire skeleton with **HRR***, which stands for* **High Resolution Rig***.*

3   **Add the bound attributes**

- **Source** the *HRRaddBoundAttr.mel* script.

- Select all the joints in the scene by selecting the *bodyJ_1* joint and then selecting **Edit** → **Select Hierarchy**.

- Execute `HRRaddBoundToAll` in the Command Line.

This will add the HRRbound attribute to every joint in the selection if it does not exist already. It also adds the name of the joint into a string attribute so that, in case the joint's name gets changed, the tool still knows which joint should be controlled.

4   **Check if the attributes were created**

- Select any joint and open its Attribute Editor.

- Under the **Extra Attributes** section, make sure the **Hrr Bound** attribute is there.

5   **Save your work**

- Save your scene as *08-boundRig_01.ma*.

The control rig

Now that the renderable bound rig has been created, you need to create an animatable version of the rig for the animators. Starting with the skeleton scene as the base, you will create an entirely new hierarchy, adding in anything needed by anyone down the pipeline.

Instead of starting from scratch and building a completely new rig, you will simply break up the original skeleton you built earlier.

Remember each individual joint chain will consist of a *JCon*, *JA*, …, to the *JEnd* joint. The *JCon* joints will take all the constraints so that the animator can cleanly add curves to the top of the joint via the *JA* joints. If there is a child chain under this chain, there will be a *JOri* joint in the parent chain for the orientation setup to work.

1   **Scene file**

- Open the scene file *07-rig_01.ma*.

2   **Breaking up the chains**

- **Source** the *breakJointChain.mel* script.

- **Select** the *neckJA_1* joint.

- **Execute** `breakJointChain` in the Command Line.

*The script will duplicate and break the chain at the selected joint. It will then add a JCon correctly to the new chain, and also zero out the **Joint Orient** of the JEnd of the parent chain break point. You will need to rename those two joints by hand.*

- **Rename** *neckJA_2* to *neckJEnd_1*.

- **Rename** *neckJA_3* to *headJCon_1*.

- Repeat the previous steps to break the hierarchy at the following joints:

  headJA_1;

  armJALf_1;

  handJALf_1;

  armJARt_1;

  handJARt_1;

  legJALf_1 (**Rename** the *JEnd* to *pelvisJEndRt_1*);

  footJALf_1;

  legJARt_1 (**Rename** the *JEnd* to *pelvisJEndRt_1*);

  footJARt_1.

- Make sure all the joints are named correctly.

3   Orient constraints

Now that the rig is completely broken up, you need to add the point and orient constraints on all chains with the automated tool used earlier so that they follow as a continuous hierarchy would.

- Execute `HRRoriConsWin` to display the **Orient Constraint Tool's** options.

- Select a *JCon* of a joint chain and then **Ctrl-select** the corresponding *JEnd* of the parent chain in the Outliner.

- In the tool window, enter a proper name in the **New Orient Constraint Name** field, such as *arm*, and then specify the proper **Name Suffix**.

- Click the **Create Orient Constraint** button.

- Repeat for all of the following joint chains.

JCon

neckJCon_1;

headJCon_1;

armJConLf_1;

armJConRt_1;

handConLf_1;

handConRt_1;

legJConLf_1;

legJConRt_1;

footJConLf_1;

footJConRt_1;

JEnd

spineJEnd_1;

neckJEnd_1;

clavJEndLf_1;

clavJEndRt_1;

armJEndLf_1;

armJEndRt_1;

pelvisJEndLf_1;

pelvisJEndRt_1;

legJEndLf_1;

legJEndRt_1;

4   **Save your scene**

- Save your scene as *08-controlRig_01.ma*.

Character hierarchy

Now that you have built your creature's rig, you need to place the nodes and chains into an easy and clean hierarchy that is standardized so that anyone can find anything they are looking for quickly and easily. It is recommended to set and use standards for every creature and make sure every animator knows how to use and find things.

Control rig hierarchy

The following steps explain how things should be organized in your control rig.

1   **Scene file**

- Open the scene file *08-controlRig_01.ma*.

2 Top node

There should be only a single top node for the creature to ensure there is no clutter in the Outliner when everything is collapsed.

```
⊟  ▱  topNodeN_1
   ⊟  ▱    globalTransAN_1
      ⊟  ▱      globalTransBN_1
         ⊟  ▱        globalTransCN_1
```

- Create an empty group and **rename** it to *topNodeN_1*.
- Lock and hide all of this node's attributes. This node should never be transformed or else it would cause double transformations and other problems.

3 Global transformation nodes

- Create three other empty groups and **rename** them *globalTransAN_1*, *globalTransBN_1* and *globalTransCN_1*.

These groups will be used as global transformation overrides. You would use these to properly place the creature in your scene by translating or rotating. This will move everything needed, including IK handles and controls.

- Parent these nodes to each other and under the top node.

- Lock and hide this node's Scale and Visibility attributes since they should only be moved or rotated.

4 Scale node

- Create an empty group and **rename** it to *scaleN_1*.

```
⊟  ▱  topNodeN_1
   ⊟  ▱    globalTransAN_1
      ⊟  ▱      globalTransBN_1
         ⊟  ▱        globalTransCN_1
            ⊟  ▱          allScaleN_1
```

This node will be used to globally scale your creature if need be.

- Parent this node under the *globalTransCN_1* node.

- Lock and hide every attribute in this node, but with the exception of the scaling attribute.

Note: Notice the name of the top node does not contain the name of the character. This is because the name of the character will eventually be added when imported or referenced into a scene.

5 **Organization node**

- Create an empty group and **rename** it to *pupPartsN_1*.

  This node is based at the origin and is meant simply for organization.

- Parent this node under the *scaleN_1* node.

- Lock and hide all attributes on this node.

```
⊟  ▱  topNodeN_1
⊟  ▱    globalTransAN_1
⊟  ▱      globalTransBN_1
⊟  ▱        globalTransCN_1
⊟  ▱          allScaleN_1
⊟  ▱            pupPartsN_1
```

6 **Pelvic override nodes**

- Create three other empty groups and **rename** them *bodyTransAN_1*, *bodyTransBN_1* and *bodyTransCN_1*.

  These nodes are located at the pelvis or center of mass of your creature. They will be used as your body translation overrides. They will allow you to pose your creature's pelvis, but will not move any IK or special controls.

- Parent these nodes to each other and under the pupPartsN_1 node.

- Lock and hide all of these nodes' attributes.

```
⊟  ▱  topNodeN_1
⊟  ▱    globalTransAN_1
⊟  ▱      globalTransBN_1
⊟  ▱        globalTransCN_1
⊟  ▱          allScaleN_1
⊟  ▱            pupPartsN_1
⊟  ▱              bodyTransAN_1
⊟  ▱                bodyTransBN_1
⊟  ▱                  bodyTransCN_1
```

7 **Skeleton node**

- Create an empty group and rename it to *skeleN_1*.

  This node is just another organizational node based at the origin. Under this node you will place all the skeletal joint chains of the creature.

- Parent this node under the *bodyTransCN_1* node.

- **Parent** all of the joint chains under this *skeleN_1* node.

- Lock and hide all this node's attributes.

```
⊟  ▱  topNodeN_1
⊟  ▱    globalTransAN_1
⊟  ▱      globalTransBN_1
⊟  ▱        globalTransCN_1
⊟  ▱          allScaleN_1
⊟  ▱            pupPartsN_1
⊟  ▱              bodyTransAN_1
⊟  ▱                bodyTransBN_1
⊟  ▱                  bodyTransCN_1
⊟  ▱                    skeleN_1
⊞  ⌇                      bodyJ_1
⊞  ⌇                      neckJCon_1
⊞  ⌇                      headJCon_1
⊞  ⌇                      armJConLf_1
⊞  ⌇                      armJConRt_1
⊞  ⌇                      handJConLf_1
⊞  ⌇                      handJConRt_1
⊞  ⌇                      legJConLf_1
⊞  ⌇                      legJConRt_1
⊞  ⌇                      footJConLf_1
⊞  ⌇                      footJConRt_1
```

8 Rig node groups

- **Create** three other empty groups and **rename** them *orientsN_1*, *ikHandlesN_1* and *controlsN_1*.

  The *orientsN_1* is for all the joint orientation group nodes for each joint chain that were created in the previous example. The *ikHandlesN_1* is the placeholder for IK handles. The *controlsN_1* is for any other rig nodes such as manipulator objects, locators that do not require any specific parents, etc.

- **Parent** these nodes under *pupPartsN_1*.

- **Lock** and hide all of these nodes' attributes.

⊟ ▱	topNodeN_1	
⊟ ▱	globalTransAN_1	
⊟ ▱	globalTransBN_1	
⊟ ▱	globalTransCN_1	
⊟ ▱	allScaleN_1	
⊟ ▱	pupPartsN_1	
⊟ ▱	bodyTransAN_1	
⊟ ▱	bodyTransBN_1	
⊟ ▱	bodyTransCN_1	
⊟ ▱	skeleN_1	
⊞ 🦴		bodyJ_1
⊞ 🦴		neckJCon_1
⊞ 🦴		headJCon_1
⊞ 🦴		armJConLf_1
⊞ 🦴		armJConRt_1
⊞ 🦴		handJConLf_1
⊞ 🦴		handJConRt_1
⊞ 🦴		legJConLf_1
⊞ 🦴		legJConRt_1
⊞ 🦴		footJConLf_1
⊞ 🦴		footJConRt_1
⊞ ▱	orientsN_1	
▱	ikHandlesN_1	
▱	controlsN_1	

Note: Since you used the orientation script in the previous exercise, you might not have to create the orientsN_1 node. Instead, simply parent the already existing node.

9 Config node

- **Create** an empty group and **rename** it to *configN_1*.

  As mentioned before, the *configN_1* node is the storage place for all custom switch controls on the creature. Anything that an animator may need for the creature that is not on a specific node should be found here.

⊟ ▱	topNodeN_1	
⊟ ▱	globalTransAN_1	
⊟ ▱	globalTransBN_1	
⊟ ▱	globalTransCN_1	
⊟ ▱	allScaleN_1	
⊟ ▱	pupPartsN_1	
⊟ ▱	bodyTransAN_1	
⊟ ▱	bodyTransBN_1	
⊟ ▱	bodyTransCN_1	
⊟ ▱	skeleN_1	
⊞ 🦴		bodyJ_1
⊞ 🦴		neckJCon_1
⊞ 🦴		headJCon_1
⊞ 🦴		armJConLf_1
⊞ 🦴		armJConRt_1
⊞ 🦴		handJConLf_1
⊞ 🦴		handJConRt_1
⊞ 🦴		legJConLf_1
⊞ 🦴		legJConRt_1
⊞ 🦴		footJConLf_1
⊞ 🦴		footJConRt_1
⊞ ▱	orientsN_1	
▱	ikHandlesN_1	
▱	controlsN_1	
▱	configN_1	

Note: Like with the orientsN_1 node, since you used the orientation script in the previous exercise, you might not have to create the configN_1 node. Instead, simply parent the already existing node as follows.

- Parent this node under the top node.

- Lock and hide every attribute in this node.

10 Model node

- Create an empty group and **rename** it to *mdlN_1*.

This node is for all the model geometry that gets bound to the different joint chains.

- Parent this under the top node.

Since most geometry will be bound, you don't want this node to move and cause double transformations, so you must place the geometry under a node that gets no animation.

- Parent the geometry of the beast under this *mdlN_1* node.

- Lock and hide every attribute in this node.

```
topNodeN_1
    globalTransAN_1
        globalTransBN_1
            globalTransCN_1
                allScaleN_1
                    pupPartsN_1
                        bodyTransAN_1
                            bodyTransBN_1
                                bodyTransCN_1
                                    skeleN_1
                                        bodyJ_1
                                        neckJCon_1
                                        headJCon_1
                                        armJConLf_1
                                        armJConRt_1
                                        handJConLf_1
                                        handJConRt_1
                                        legJConLf_1
                                        legJConRt_1
                                        footJConLf_1
                                        footJConRt_1
                                    orientsN_1
                                    ikHandlesN_1
                                    controlsN_1
                configN_1
                mdlN_1
```

11 Extra node

- Create an empty group and **rename** it to *xtraN_1*.

This node will be for any extra node that the creature rig will need. Examples would be nodes such as blend shape geometry, specially driven controls and joints, etc.

- Parent this under the top node.

- Lock and hide all this node's attributes.

```
⊟  ▱  topNodeN_1
   ⊟  ▱    globalTransAN_1
      ⊟  ▱     globalTransBN_1
         ⊟  ▱      globalTransCN_1
            ⊟  ▱       allScaleN_1
               ⊟  ▱        pupPartsN_1
                  ⊟  ▱          bodyTransAN_1
                     ⊟  ▱           bodyTransBN_1
                        ⊟  ▱            bodyTransCN_1
                           ⊟  ▱             skeleN_1
                              ⊞  ⚉              bodyJ_1
                              ⊞  ⚉              neckJCon_1
                              ⊞  ⚉              headJCon_1
                              ⊞  ⚉              armJConLf_1
                              ⊞  ⚉              armJConRt_1
                              ⊞  ⚉              handJConLf_1
                              ⊞  ⚉              handJConRt_1
                              ⊞  ⚉              legJConLf_1
                              ⊞  ⚉              legJConRt_1
                              ⊞  ⚉              footJConLf_1
                              ⊞  ⚉              footJConRt_1
                           ⊞  ▱             orientsN_1
                              ▱             ikHandlesN_1
                              ▱             controlsN_1
                     ▱        configN_1
   ⊞  ▱        mdlN_1
      ▱        xtraN_1
```

Standardized hierarchy for the creature control rig

12 Save your scene

- Save your scene as *08-controlRig_02.ma*.

Bound rig hierarchy

The following steps explain how things should be organized in your bound rig.

1 Scene file

- Open the scene file *08-boundRig_01.ma*.

2 Top node

- Create an empty group and **rename** it to *topNodeN_1*.

- Lock and hide all attributes in this node.

3 Global transformation node

- Create another empty group and **rename** it to *globalTransN_1*.

- Parent this node to the *topNodeN_1*.

- Parent the skeleton under the *globalTransN_1* node.

4 Model group

- Create another empty group and **rename** it to *mdIN_1*.

- Lock and hide all of this node's attributes.

- Parent this node to the *topNodeN_1*.

- Parent all the geometry under the *mdIN_1* node.

5 Final hierarchy

The following image shows what your hierarchy should look like at this point.

6 Save your scene

- Save your scene as *08-boundRig_02.ma*.

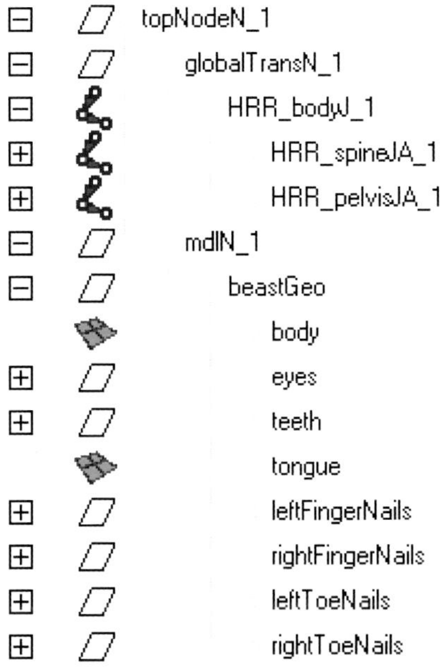

The scapula

One thing that is recommended to add into a humanoid creature is a semi-automatic scapula with override control, in case the animator wants to animate over it if need be.

The scapula is a simple setup showing the power of the aim constraint. With aim constraints you have the ability to have an *up* object, giving you the power to control the orientation based on another moving object.

Control rig scapula setup

To create this setup, you should first create it for the control rig, and then use a duplicate of that joint in the bound rig.

topNodeN_1
  globalTransN_1
    HRR_bodyJ_1
      HRR_spineJA_1
      HRR_pelvisJA_1
    mdIN_1
      beastGeo
        body
        eyes
        teeth
        tongue
        leftFingerNails
        rightFingerNails
        leftToeNails
        rightToeNails

Standardized hierarchy for the creature bound rig

1 Scene file

- Open the scene file *08-controlRig_02.ma*.

2 Add the scapula

- From the *front* view, draw two joints as follows:

131

The parent scapula joint should be at the point where the clavicle and scapula touch each other under the skin. The end joint should be placed at the bottom tip of where the scapula would be.

- Rename the joint chain with the *scapula* prefix using the *templateSkeleton* script.

- Parent the *scapula* chain to the *clavJA_1* joint.

3   Create the scapula node

- Execute the `breakJointChain` command in the Command Line.

- Rename the *JCon* and *JEnd* appropriately.

- Create a locator and snap it to the end joint of the scapula.

- Rename the locator to *scapAimAtLocLf_1*.

- Parent it to the *spineJC_1* joint.

- Translate the *scapulaJEnd_1* to about half its Translate X value.

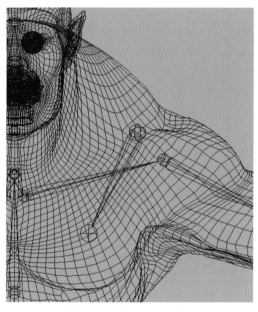

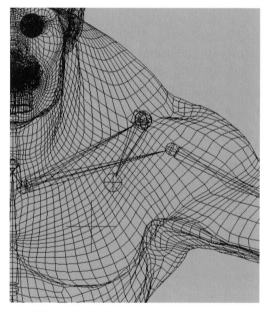

The scapula joint chain location   The scapula aim locator and the shorter end joint

- Create another **locator** and **parent** it to *spineJEnd_1*.

- Rename this locator to *scapAimUpLoc_1*.

- Zero the **Translate** and **Rotate** attributes of the locator so that it jumps at the location of the spine end joint.

- Translate the locator toward the back in **negative Y** and up in **negative X** until it is just at the edge of the model surface.

When you look at the locator in the front view, the locator should be right in the center of the beast.

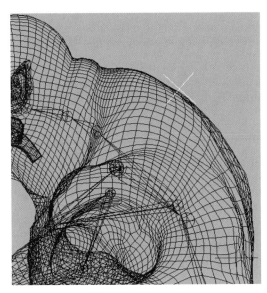

The locator placement

4   Set up the scapula constraints

- Point constrain the *scapJCon_1* to the *clavScapJEnd_1* joint.

- Select the *scapAimAtLoc_1* and then Ctrl-select the *scapJCon_1* from the Outliner.

- Create an **aim constraint** with the following options:

  Maintain Offset to **On**;

  worldUpType set to **objectup**;

  worldUpObject set to *scapAimUpLoc_1*.

5   Make the right side scapula setup

- Repeat the previous steps to make the right side scapula setup.

> *Tip:*   *You can mirror the joint chain and use the same scapAimUpLoc_1 for both setups.*

6   Save your work

- Save your scene as *08-controlRig_03.ma*.

Bound rig scapula setup

You will now export a duplicate of the scapula joint chain and import it in the bound rig.

1   Export the scapula joint

- Select the *scapJALf_1* joint and the *scapJARt_1* and then **duplicate** them.

- Press **Shift+p** to **unparent** the new joint chains.

- Select File → **Export Selection** → ❏ and set **File Type** to **mayaAscii**.

- Click on the **Export Selection** button and export the file as *scapula_export.ma*.

2   Scene file

- Close the control rig file **without saving** your changes.

- Open the scene file *08-boundRig_02.ma*.

3   Import the scapula joint chain

- Select **File** → **Import** and choose *scapula_export.ma*.

You should see the scapula joint chains taking their place in the geometry.

- Parent the *scapJALf_2* to the *HRR_clavJALf_1*.

- Parent the *scapJARt_2* to the *HRR_clavJARt_1*.

- Rename the two new joint chains with the proper prefix and suffix.

4   Add the bound attributes

- Select all the new scapula joints.

- Execute `HRRaddBoundToAll` in the Command Line.

5   Save your work

- Save your scene as *08-boundRig_03.ma*.

Adding the control attributes

Since you added hidden attributes to the bound rig joints, you need to add some to the control rig as well. This will add both the hidden attribute and the name of the joint to be driven.

> **Note:**   The tool will automatically add the HRR_ prefix the name needs.

1   Scene file

- Open the scene file *08-controlRig_03.ma*.

2   Use the automated script

- Source the *HRRaddControlAttrs.mel*.

- Execute `HRRaddControlAttrTo` in the Command Line.

This will find all the joints and add the new hidden attributes, as long as they don't contain JCon or JOri.

- You can see the new attributes on the joints in the **Extra Attributes** section of the Attribute Editor.

3   Save your work

- Save your scene as *08-controlRig_04.ma*.

> **Note:** *You will be connecting the bound rig to the control rig later in this lesson, once it is ready to be animated.*

Extra controls

Every animator and studio is going to be different with what they want and need for controls in a rig. That is not even including the different needs for every creature for every shot. Just like the rest of this book's techniques, each of these steps can be customized to achieve different end results.

This section will not cover how to create different types of controls, but that doesn't mean that you can't experiment and add your own favorite control into the control rig. In fact, you are encouraged to do so!

Some of these controls may be FK/IK control switching, eye aim constraints, reverse feet control, selection manipulators, wrist twists, auto clavicles, IK splines, etc. The list of different manipulation devices that can be added is numerous.

> **Note:** *You can find a simple IK/FK rig in the support files under the name 08-IKhandles.ma. The IK/FK blending attributes are located on the configN_1 node.*

Lock and hide attributes

Before you are finished with any rig, always make sure that there are no attributes open in the rig that may accidentally get keyframed. Lock and hide any superfluous attributes on all joints and nodes that you don't want anyone to edit.

Perhaps the fastest way to do this is by highlighting attributes and right-clicking in the Channel Box, then selecting **Lock and Hide Selected**.

> **Tip:** *There are several ways of doing the locking and hiding of attributes and you should strongly consider speeding up the task with MEL scripting.*

Conclusion

You have now completed two different rigs, one with controls for animation and another that will be animated by connections to the animation rig and eventually used for rendering.

In the next lesson, you will bind the geometry of the beast to its skeleton, thus allowing it to deform along with the animation.

Lesson 09 *Skinning*

In this lesson, you will make the beast deform correctly with the skeleton you built in the last lesson. You will use smooth skinning and precise weighting. With proficient joint placement and skillful weighting you can get any creature to deform quite well for most purposes.

In this lesson you will learn the following:

- How to do the initial skinning;

- How to paint skin weights;

- How to test deformations;

- How to lock skin weights;

- About trouble spots;

- Wrist twist setup;

- How to prune small weights;

- How to mirror skin weights.

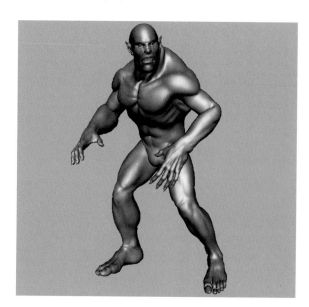

The skinned bound rig

Skinning theory

Skinning a character means attaching the skin geometry to the skeleton so that it deforms along when animating. In order to deform the geometry properly, you must edit the influence of each bone on the skin and adjust it so that it provides the best deformation possible.

If your model is polygonal and has multiple pieces, it would be easier for you to make a continuous version, then bind and weight that version and then transfer the weights to the multiple models with the *Copy Weights Tool*. This is because painting weights works much better when you can paint over seams on a unique model.

> **Note:** You can use the Skin → Edit Smooth Skin → Substitute Geometry in Maya 7 software rather than using the Copy Weight Tool.

> **Note:** *When you have a seam between the two surfaces and you don't want that seam to open when deforming, you must make sure to have the exact same weight values on both sides of the seam. Making sure each corresponding point on either side of a seam have the exact same weighting value is very difficult to achieve by hand.*

If you need extra deformations that skinning alone won't provide, using blend shapes or clusters on top of the bound skin is the easiest method without having access to higher level deformation systems such as muscle deformations and sliding skin.

The initial bind

When binding a model, you can set the amount of joints that can potentially affect the same geometric point. For starters, it is much easier to deal with an initial bind that has as few influences per geometric point as possible. This will give a coarser default skinning and you will have to refine all weighting, but you will most likely end up editing all skin weights later anyway.

1   Scene file

- Open the scene file *08-boundRig_03.ma*.

2   Bind the beast

- Select all joints but the *JEnd* and the *bodyJ_1* joints.

- Shift-select the beast's skin geometry.

- **Select Skin → Bind Skin → Smooth Bind → ❑.**

- In the option window, set the following:

  Bind to to **Selected Joints**;

  Max Influences to **1**;

  Maintain Max Influence to **1**.

- Click on the **Bind Skin** button.

  The beast's skin is now bound to the skeleton with default coarse weights.

3   Change the Max influences

Now that the initial bind is set, you will need to reset the max influences to their default value so that you can paint some nice falloffs at articulations between the influences. To do so without resetting all the weights automatically, you must first lock the weighting on all the joints.

- **Source** the script *tglSkinHold.mel*.

- Execute `tglSkinHold` in the Command Line.

Doing so will display a small window that allows you to lock or unlock the weights of geometry.

- Select the beast's geometry and then click on the **Hold ON** button.

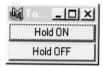

The tglSkinHold UI

- With the skin still selected, choose **Skin → Edit Smooth Skin → Set Max Influences**.

- In the option window, set the **Max Influences** to **5** and click the **Apply and Close** button.

4 Bind the other geometry

You can now bind the eyes, nails and inner mouth.

5 Save your work

- Save your scene as *09-boundrig_04.ma*.

> **Tip:** For geometry that has just one influence, instead of parenting it you can bind it. The refresh will be a little slower than if you were directly parenting it, but this way, the model hierarchy is still kept the way the modeler gave it to you.

Weighting

Weighting is the process of editing the influences of each joint for each point in the bound geometry. If your model is symmetrical, you can weight only half the influences and then mirror the weights.

The weighting process can be roughly described by three stages:

- First, you need to assign coarse weighting to all the influences in order to start with a good base.

- Second, you do a general painting pass designing the influence maps to have adequate deformation based on the underlying muscles and bones.

> **Tip:** For reference while weighting a creature, use muscle groupings and anatomy as guides, just as you did for modeling and skeletal placements.

- Lastly, (but the longest step), you fine-tune every influence, making sure that they smoothly and adequately deform the geometry. Again, if your model is symmetrical, you can refine only half the influences and then mirror the weights.

At this stage, you should be able to bend every joint to quasi-extreme rotations and still see good deformations.

> **Note:** When skinning, don't be afraid to create creases and folds in flexible areas when weighting. Also, don't limit yourself to putting influence only in the bone area, since flesh and muscles can affect different parts of the model.

Throughout the weighting process, use the `tglSkinHold` tool to first hold all influences and then unlock the weights of the joints that you are currently editing. This is especially true when finalizing the skinning of your model.

> **Note:** While influences are held, you cannot edit them in any way. Be careful to unlock the proper joints since the edited weights might end up on the wrong joint.

Following is a typical workflow when painting weights:

- Use the **Paint Skin Weights Tool**, found under **Skin → Edit Smooth Skin → Paint Skin Weights Tool → ❑** to edit the **weight maps.**

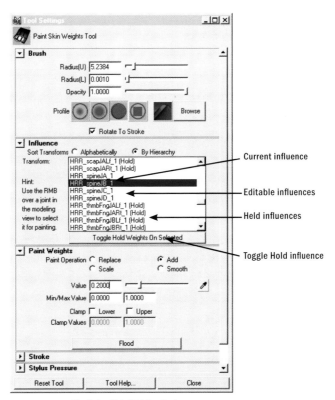

The Paint Skin Weights Tool

- Hold all the influences of the skin.

- Unhold a specific influence and also those that are the neighbor influences to the region you want to edit.

- Try to always **Add** weights with a **Value** of **0.2** for instance.

*When you **Add** weights to an influence, ensure that you are removing weights from another place in order to add them to the current bone. If you **Replace** weights with a low value, you might not always know where the weights are being reassigned.*

Tip: *Hold down b and click+drag in the viewport to change the radius of your paintbrush.*

- Do not use the **Smooth** feature of the Paint Tool until you are satisfied with the weighting of your entire character.

Smoothing the weights too early in the weighting process increases the chances of having weights assigned to incorrect influences, which will be difficult to solve later on.

- Repeat as needed.

Tip: *Consider using a pen and tablet when painting weights.*

Another technique to use while weighting tricky areas is to select just the vertices that you wish to edit, and then go into the Paint Skin Weights Tool. By doing this, you will be allowed to edit only those points, thus preventing accidental editing.

Note: *You can watch the movie called paintingWeights.mov to learn about painting weights.*

Test the weighting

In older versions of Maya software, you had to either exit the Paint Tool or keyframe simple animation in order to test the skinning while weighting. Now, you can use the interactive **Rotate Tool** feature of the Paint Skin Weights Tool as you are painting weights. This feature allows you to rotate the current bone to see how it deforms the skin.

The following explains how to use this feature:

- Select the influence for which you want to test rotations in the **Paint Skin Weights Tool**.

- **MMB+click** in the viewport.

*Doing so will enable the **Rotate Tool**.*

- **MMB-click+drag** in the viewport to change the rotation of the influence.

*The joint will rotate according to the current camera angle. To rotate the joint in a different way, simply rotate the camera around and **MMB-click+drag** again.*

- Re-enable the **Paint Skin Weight Tool** by clicking anywhere in the viewport.

- To reset the rotations of the joint, **RMB-click** in the viewport and select **Assume Preferred Angle**.

Note: You must have set the preferred angle at least once for this last step to work properly.

- Another option for resetting the rotations of all joints is to select **Skin → Go to Bind Pose**.

Trouble areas

There are usually several problematic areas when weighting a model that will give trouble to any setup artist. There is no way to describe the perfect weight map, but following are some images that you can use as reference.

Shoulders

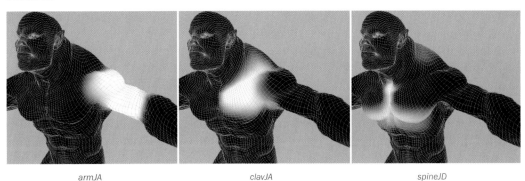

armJA   clavJA   spineJD

Hips

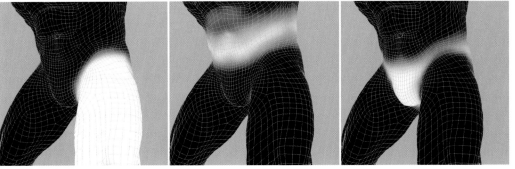

legJA   spineJA   pelvisJA

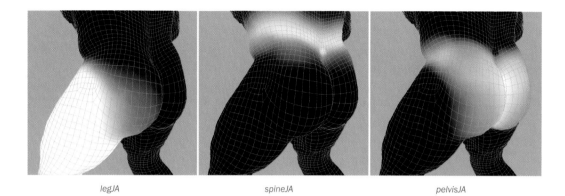

| legJA | spineJA | pelvisJA |

Movie: *Open the scene file 09-boundRig_05.ma to have a look at the weighting for the entire body.*

Twist bones

In the human body, the rotation of the wrist is spread across the entire forearm due to the radius and ulna bones twisting.

Note: *The same type of spreading along a bone is also true elsewhere on the body (but less apparent), not only because of bones twisting, but because the flesh is stretching when rotating a bone on its X-axis.*

If you open the file *09-boundRig_05.ma* from the previous example, you will see that the wrist reacts correctly when bent on its Y and Z axes, but if you rotate it on its X-axis, the binding creases and breaks.

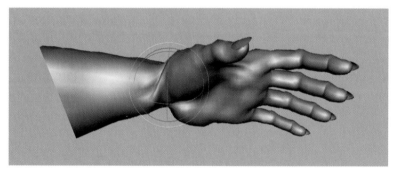

Bad deformation when rotating the wrist on its X-axis

To fix this, you will need to add another joint, a *twist* joint, which will be allowed to only twist on its X-axis, thus spreading the deformation along the forearm. This new bone will also be completely automated by connecting the X rotation from the wrist to its own X rotation.

You could also solve the problem shown here by using more than one joint to split up the rotation of an area. This simply requires you to evenly space the joints down the bone, smooth out the weighting of each of these joints and then create a connection or an expression that will split the rotation proportionally across the bones.

The following will show you how to set-up a twist bone for the wrist.

1 Scene file

- Open the scene file *09-boundRig_05.ma*.

2 Create the twist bone

- Duplicate the *armJBLf* joint.

- Delete every child so that you have only a single joint.

- Parent the new joint to the *armJBLf* joint.

- Translate this joint on its **Translate X** axis and place it in the middle of the forearm.

- Rename the joint to *wristTwistJALf_1*.

3 Connect the twist joint

Since this will be a single twist joint setup, you will directly connect the wrist X rotation to the twist joint.

- Select **Windows → General Editors → Connection Editor**.

- On the **left** side, load the *handJALf* joint.

- On the **right** side, load the *wristTwistJALf* joint.

- Connect the Rotate X attribute from the wrist to the Rotate X attribute of the twist joint.

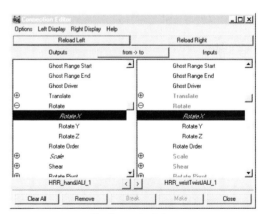

The Connection Editor

> **Note:** *If you have a multi twist joint setup, you can create a multiply/divide utility node to distribute a fraction of the rotation to each joint.*

4 Create the other twist joint

Use the same technique described above to create the right arm twist joint.

5 Add the influences to the skin

In this scenario, since you created the twist joints after binding the character, you will need to add the joints as influences to the skin.

- Select both twist joints and then **Shift-select** the skinned geometry.

- Select **Skin** → **Edit Smooth Skin** → **Add Influence** → o.

- In the option window, set Lock Weights to **On** and the Default Weight to **0.0**.

Doing so will prevent the new influences from being assigned weights, which could potentially affect the weighting you did earlier.

- Click the Add button.

6 Paint the weights of the twist joints

- Open the **Paint Skin Weights Tool**.

- Use `tglSkinHold` to lock all the skin influences.

- Unhold the *armJBLf* joint.

This is where you will take the influence from.

- Scroll at the very bottom of the influence list and **unhold** the *wristTwistJALf* influence.

- Select the **Add** option with a **Value** of **0.2** and then the **Smooth** option to paint the weights as follows:

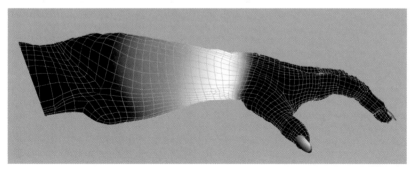

The twist bone influence

> **Tip:** You do not need to paint the weights of the right twist bone since the weights will be mirrored later in this lesson.

7 Save your work

- Save your scene as *09-boundRig_06.ma*.

The twist joint solution for the problem encountered here really helped resolve the crease created at the wrist, but it also brought in a new problem. This new problem is caused by standard skinning deformations that occur when you twist a joint on its **Rotate X** attribute too much. Doing such a rotation tends to cause the geometry to twist (like a candy unwrapping) or *implode*. One of the multiple ways of fixing this is by adding in corrective blend shapes to counter the implosion of the geometry, which will be covered in the next lesson.

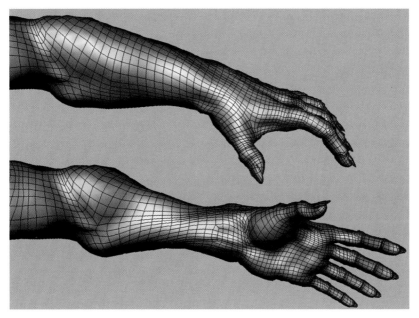

Effect of twisting a joint on its X-axis too much

Prune weights

When skinning a model, it is almost inevitable to have small influences that you don't want on points of geometry. The best way of adjusting this is to prune the small weights on your bound skin. Pruning is a way of cleaning the weights that are smaller than a certain value. Once the weights are cleaner, if needed, you can continue editing the weights. You can also reuse the **Prune Tool** as many times as you want during the weighting process.

1 Pruning a skin

- Select the bound skin.

- Unhold all the skin weights.

- Select **Skin → Edit Smooth Skin → Prune Small Weights →** ❑.

- In the option window, set the Prune Below value to a small value.

Setting a value of **0.01** *will prune the weights that are less that* **1%**. *Usually the default value works well.*

- Click on the **Prune** button.

> **Tip:** *If you notice that even after pruning the weights there are still unwanted small influences around the geometry when moving a joint, try increasing the pruning value. If the value gets too high, you might have to smooth some of the weights again.*

Component Editor

If you encounter areas where a few vertices are not behaving like you want, consider using the **Window → General Editors → Component Editor**. This editor allows you to manually set the weights of vertices to their influences.

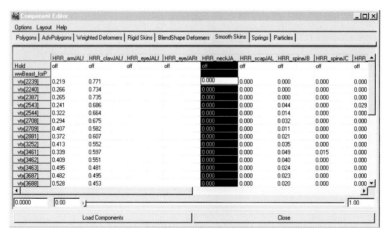

The Component Editor

> **Tip:** *You can zero an entire unwanted influence simply by selecting its column and setting it to 0.*

Mirror weights

Another thing you will find very useful with a symmetrical model such as the beast, is the fact that you can work on only half of the model and then mirror the weights over to the other side.

1   Mirroring weights

- After editing all the weights for half the model, **unhold** all the skin weights.

- Select **Skin** → **Edit Smooth Skin** → **Mirror Skin Weights** → ❑.

- In the option window, set Mirror Across to the YZ plane, then set the Direction of the mirroring depending on which side of the model you painted.

- Click on the Mirror button.

2   Repeat

Use the **Mirror Skin Weights Tool** as much as you require. For instance, you can use it while you are progressing with the skinning to see the proper deformation on the spine, or you can use it just before calling the skinned model final.

Tip: *Of course, before doing actions or using a tool that affects the entire character, it is strongly recommended to save. Good setup artists always save often just to be safe.*

Movie: *The final scene file from the support files is called 09-boundRig_06.ma.*

Conclusion

In this lesson, you learned how to efficiently skin a model. Using the different techniques and tips shown here, you will be able to have the best deformations possible for your character using basic smooth binding.

In the next lesson, you will build a low resolution model for the control rig.

Lesson 10 *Final touches*

In this lesson, you will use a partially automated process to create a low resolution proxy model to be used with the control rig. Having such a low resolution model will allow the animators to keep their minds focused on the movement of the character and also have a decent playback speed while animating.

As well, you will learn how to use influence objects and create corrective blend shapes to raise the level of deformation on the high resolution model.

In this lesson you will learn the following:

- A fast way to build a low resolution model;

- How to connect the bound rig to the control rig;

- How to use influence objects;

- How to create corrective blend shapes.

The posed low resolution control rig

Low resolution model

Before you can hand over the control rig to the animators, you first need to insert a low resolution version of the bound model so that they can get an idea of what the character looks like and still have a decent playback rate when animating.

You will now use a partially automated MEL script that will help you model the low resolution proxy geometry.

1   Scene file

- Open the scene file *09-boundRig_06.ma*.

This scene contains the bound high resolution geometry from the last lesson.

2   Source the script

- **Source** the script *createLoRez.mel* from the support files.

- **Execute** `createLoRez` in the Command Line.

Doing so will open the tool's option window.

3 Create the low geometry

- Select the beast's bound skin.

- Click on the **Create Lo Rez By SkinCluster** button.

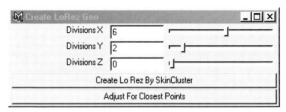

The createLoRez window

This will create polygonal cylinders with the subdivisions set in the option window for every joint influence in the currently selected skin cluster. It also parents each cylinder under the joint and finds its correct length.

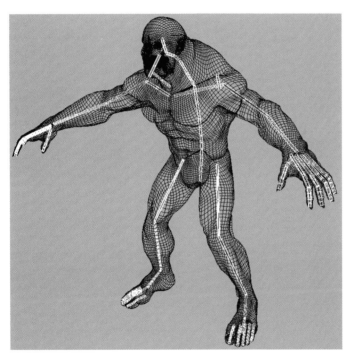

The initial low resolution geometry is created automatically per joint in the skin cluster

4 Adjust the geometry

- Turn **Off** the **Joint Selection Mask** in the Status Line at the top of the interface, then **RMB-click** on the skin and select **Actions → Template**.

Doing so will help you select the cylinders.

- **Scale** each of the cylinders on their **Y** and **Z** axes to make them closer to the volume of the skin geometry.

You don't have to do this step perfectly. Roughing out the volume of skin geometry is enough for the script to then adjust the low resolution geometry to the high resolution geometry.

Tip: *When using the* **Scale Tool**, *simply hold down* **Ctrl** *and* **click+drag** *on the X-axis to proportionally scale on both the* **Y** *and* **Z** *axes.*

5 Refine the geometry

- Select all the cylinders, then **Shift-select** the bound skin geometry.

- Click on the **Adjust For Closest Points** button of the *createLoRez* window.

  The tool will work for a couple of minutes, looking at each vertex in the low resolution geometry and snapping it to the closest point it can find in the last selected skin geometry.

- **Edit** the low resolution model further to make it as close as possible to the high resolution model.

The roughly scaled cylinders

6 Export the model

- Select all the low resolution cylinders, then press **Ctrl+g** to group them together.

- Press **Shift+p** to **unparent** the new group from the bound rig's hierarchy.

- Select **File → Export Selection** to export the low resolution model to a file.

7 Import for the control rig

- Close *09-boundRig_06.ma* without saving.

- Open the scene file *08-controlRig_04.ma*.

- Select **File → Import** and import the low resolution model you just exported.

- **Reparent** every cylinder to its corresponding joint in the control rig skeleton.

- **Delete** the high resolution models.

The refined low resolution geometry

8   Save your work

- Save your work as *10-controlRig_05.ma*.

Connecting the rigs

Now that the control rig and bound rig are complete, you can go through an example where you will connect the bound rig to a posed control rig. By using the workflow shown throughout this project, connecting the rigs is only a matter of executing a MEL script.

The following example shows how to connect two rigs that are imported in the same scene file.

The posed control rig

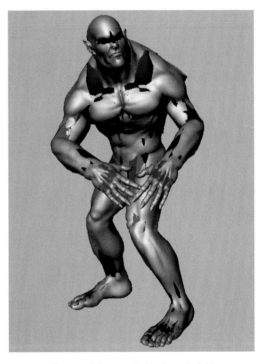

The bound rig connected to the control rig

1   Control rig

- In a new scene file, select **File** → **Import** → ❒.

- Turn Off the Use Namespaces checkbox.

- **Set Resolve** all nodes with this string: CONTROL.

- **Click** the Import button and browse for th**e** *10-controlRig_05.ma*.

2   Pose the control rig

- **Translate** the control rig and **pose** it as you would like.

3 Bound rig

- Select **File** → **Import** → ☐.

- Turn Off the Use Namespaces checkbox.

- **Set Resolve** all nodes with this string: BOUND.

- **Click** the Import button and browse for the *09-boundRig_06.ma*.

4 Connect the rigs

- **Source** the *HRRconnectControl.mel* script.

- Select the *CONTROL_topNodeN_1* and then **Ctrl-select** the *BOUND_topNodeN_1* in the Outliner.

- **Execute** `HRRconnectControlFromTo` in the Command Line.

You should see the bound rig snap onto the control rig. From now on, the bound rig will do whatever the control rig does.

5 Update the control rig

Try moving and animating the control rig to see how the bound rig reacts.

Tip: *It will be easier for you to select the control rig by placing the bound rig on a layer and setting this layer to Reference.*

6 Save your work

- Save your scene as *10-connected_01.ma*.

Influence objects

Influence objects are usually objects other than joints, intended to deform a bound surface. They can also be surfaces and use geometry components to deform a surface. Doing so allows you to create a deforming object, which in turn can deform a skinned surface.

Influence objects are extremely memory intensive and the more points you have in your model, the more memory is needed per influence. The memory adds exponentially as you add more and more muscles into the bound skin.

You can use influence objects to solve trouble areas of deformation or to mimic muscle deformations. Such set-up can produce impressive results, but will increase memory usage and file size.

Note: *It is possible to create a muscle system to reproduce a physically accurate muscle rig and to preserve volume and deform your model correctly, but it is not recommended to use this in any production environment unless you know exactly what you are doing.*

1   Scene file

- Open the scene file *10-arm.ma*.

This scene contains only the skinned arm of the character.

2   Create a muscle

- **Create** a NURBS cylinder with **4 spans** and **4 sections**.

- **Rename** the cylinder to *bicep*.

- **Edit** it to create a bicep shape.

3   Freeze the muscle

- Select **Modify → Freeze Transformations** and then **Edit → Delete by Type History** for the muscle.

4   Insert the influence object

- With the shoulder joint selected, select **Skin → Go to Bind Pose**.

- Select the arm skin, then **Shift-select** the muscle geometry.

- Select **Skin → Edit Smooth Skin → Add Influence → ❑**.

- Make sure **Lock Weights** is turned **On** and that Default Weight is set to **0.0**.

- Click on the **Add** button.

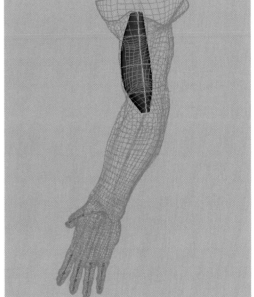

The basic NURBS muscle

The muscle is now an influence of the arm skin, but does not have any influences assigned yet. You will add influence as soon as the muscle is set-up properly.

5   Bind the muscle

- **Smooth bind** the muscle to the arm joints so that it follows the rig when animated.

- **Test** the deformation of the muscle when rotating the forearm joint.

The muscle is currently not bulging as the forearm bends.

6   Set Driven Keys

There are several ways to get the muscle to bulge as the forearm bends. A simple technique is to use Set Driven Keys.

- Select all the CVs of the muscle.

- Select **Animate** → **Set Driven Key** → **Set** → ❒.

The CVs are loaded as the driven objects.

- **Highlight** the **xValue**, **yValue** and **zValue** attributes.

Those attributes will be driven to change the shape of the muscle as the forearm bends.

- Select the forearm joint, then click on the **Load Driver** button.

- Highlight **rotateZ** as the driving attribute.

- With the arm in its default position, click the **Key** button to set the initial keyframe on the CVs.

- **Rotate** the forearm in the desired bent position.

- **Tweak** the position of the muscle CVs until you get the desired bulged shape.

- Click the **Key** button again to set the bulged position of the muscle.

7 Test the muscle

Test out the rotations on the forearm to see how the muscle is bulging.

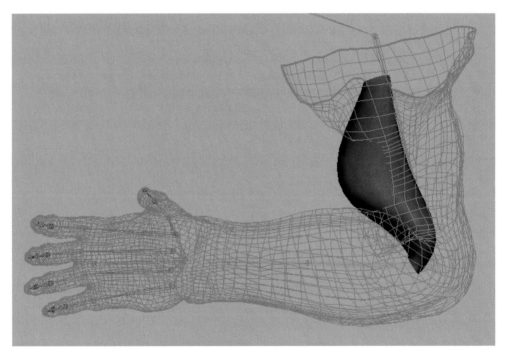

The bulged muscle

8   Add influence

- Open the **Paint Skin Weights Tool** with the arm skin selected.

- Scroll at the bottom of the list and highlight the *bicep* muscle influence.

- Toggle **Off** the **Hold Weights On Selected**.

- Paint on the arm to add some influence at the bicep area.

The influence of the bicep on the arm skin

9   Set-up the influence to use components

At this point, if you try to bend the arm, you will not see any effect on the skin. This is because, by default, when you insert an influence to a skin, it is set to use the pivot of that influence to determine the movements of the vertices. In this case, you need the CVs of the muscle to influence the skin. The following shows how to do this.

- Select the arm skin.

- Under the **Inputs** section of the Channel Box, highlight the *skinCluster* of the arm.

- Set **Use Components** to **On**.

When bending the arm, you will now see the arm skin follow the muscle deformation.

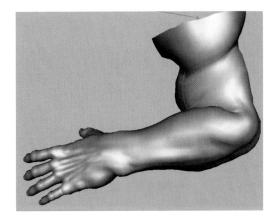

The deformed skin using an influence object

10   Save your work

- The final scene for this example is called *10-influence_01.ma*.

This example is oriented toward the concepts behind influence objects, but you are not limited to this. It might be better for customization to use other deformation techniques such as blend shapes on the muscle rather than keyframed animation. You might also want to add jiggling to the muscle to increase the realism of the deformation. You should experiment a lot with this feature before attempting to use it in production.

Note: If you use the multiple rig technique, the bound rig with muscles can be in its own separate file and can be hooked up onto the control rig as needed. Using the muscle rig only when required throughout production will save you time in the end.

Corrective blend shapes

Standard weighting of a character can only get you so far before you need to take it to the next level. The best way to implement subtleties of muscle deformation and volume preservation is to use corrective blend shapes. Blend shapes can give you much more control over the shape of the skin, allowing you to sculpt exactly what the skin deformation lacks in a certain pose.

Tip: Some of the things you would want to think about setting up are positive and negative twists of the upper arms, forearm and legs, as well as things like muscle bulges, etc.

Note: During production, weighting tweaks or specific blend shape fixes can be done on a per shot basis. Most characters are not perfect for all occasions by default, since they were set-up for general purposes. Watch out for trying to create too many blend shape fixes beforehand; most likely they will need to be tweaked on a per shot basis.

1 **Scene file**

- Open the scene file *10-arm.ma*.

This scene contains only the skinned arm of the character.

- **Rotate** the forearm joint by **90 degrees**.

Notice the bicep and forearm will lose volume and interpenetrate.

2 **Duplicate the arm**

You will now use a MEL script to duplicate the arm to be used as the blend shapes for when the elbow bends.

- **Source** the script *hyperRealCorrectiveShape.mel*.

This script will help you throughout the process of creating the corrective blend shapes.

- **Execute** *hyperRealCorrectiveShapeWin* in the Command Line.

This will bring up the script helper window.

- Select the arm geometry in the bent pose.

- Click on the **Clean Duplicate** button in the *hyperRealCorrectiveShape* window.

- **Move** the new shape to the side.

- **Rename** the geometry to *armCorrectiveShape*.

Note: *Do not freeze the transformations of the duplicate geometry.*

3   Sculpt the arm

Use the **Sculpt Geometry Tool** to sculpt the *armB* geometry to achieve the proper arm shape. Bulge the biceps and the triceps, and refine the interpenetrating geometry.

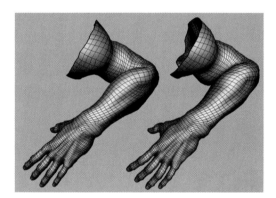
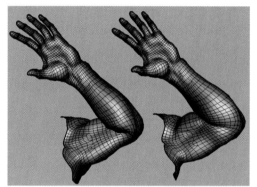

The original and corrected shapes

4   Blend shapes

- Select the *armCorrectiveShape*, then **shift-select** the *original arm*.

- Click the **Apply Shape** button in the *hyperRealCorrectiveShape* window.

*This will create a parallel blend shape node on the original arm and set the original bent arm attribute to -**1** and the bent armCorrectiveShape attribute to **1**. Doing so basically voids the bending difference between the shapes and the original arm, and then applies only the difference that you specifically modeled in the Step 3.*

5   View the results

When the original arm is in the bent position, you will only see that its shape is fixed, but if you rotate the forearm back to its original unbent position, you will notice that the arm takes a strange shape.

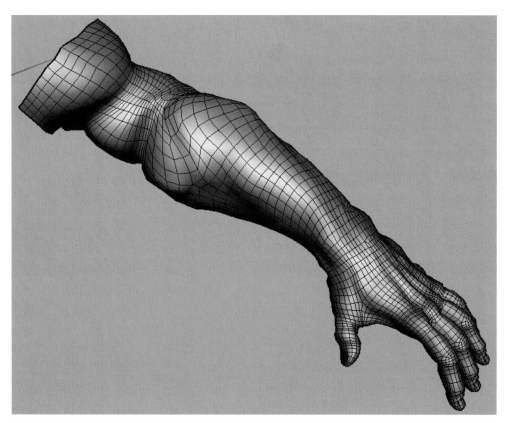

The unbent arm

6   Set Driven Keys

Now use Set Driven Keys on the arm's *parallelBlender.w[1]* in order to have the corrective blend shape at **0.0** when the arm is straight and then turn it to **1.0** when the arm is bent at **90 degrees**.

> **Note:** By default, Set Driven Keys animation curves are linear. It is recommended to change the animation curve to be flat in order to prevent snapping of the blend shape movement.

7   Save your work

- Save your scene as *10-blendshape_01.ma*.

- If you need to make corrections to the corrective blend shape, simply delete the *parallelBlender* from the original arm and go back to **Step 3**.

> **Note:** In the hyperRealCorrectiveShape window, there is also a button labeled **Select Model, Go To Pose**. This button allows you to go back to the exact same pose on the arm as when you first duplicated it to create the corrective blend shape. This is useful when you need to recreate the blend shape and need the original arm to be in the exact same position.

Conclusion

Now that you have learned the basics of rigging a biped creature such as the beast, don't be afraid to experiment with your own needs and learn from others. Remember the key rule is to keep every rig as simple as possible; this is usually the best in the long run.

In the next project, you will explore hyper-real facial rigging.

Facial
Project Three

In Project Three, you are going to
experiment using effective, flexible and
efficient techniques for creating hyper-real
facial deformations. With an emphasis
on combining rigging techniques to
achieve fully realistic control, this project
will explore the rigging process from
the concept stage through to pipeline
integration. You will learn strategies
for creating realistic creature and
character facial rigs with the following
key considerations: anatomy, realism,
animation and rendering simplicity.

Lesson 11 *Details*

In this lesson, you will begin the process of adding facial animation capabilities to the beast. You will first review facts about the human face and then examine techniques and approaches for setting up a hyper-real facial rig.

In this lesson you will learn the following:

- About the face;

- About facial muscles and skin deformation;

- The importance of having a good topology.

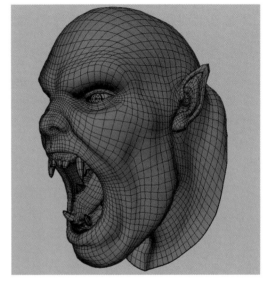

The example beast's facial topology

The amazing face

The face is the single most expressive, complex and recognizable feature of almost any living being. The amazingly wide range of emotions, ideas and suggestions that even a subtle change in facial expression can communicate are almost as broad and powerful as the spoken language that it articulates. Millions of years of evolution have trained human beings to quickly and easily recognize and read the expressions of the face. The meaning of a spoken word can be completely redefined through the subtle change of facial expressions during speech.

With over forty free floating muscles intertwined along the bones of the jaw and the skull, the human face can produce literally thousands upon thousands of uniquely identifiable expressions and phonetic shapes.

The most important thing to remember about the face is that it naturally conveys emotion to its audience, therefore quite easily sending the viewer into a state of suspended disbelief. A properly rigged hyper-realistic facial setup goes far beyond a few modeled blend shapes, and attempts to enter into a new realm of potential motion and rendering capabilities. Of course, very careful skill must be taken when animating, lighting and shading the character as well, but without the rig tying it all together, none of the rest would be possible.

Challenges

It is nearly impossible in the current computer industry to build an analytical model of something as complex as the human face, and engineer it in such a way that it is capable of a broad range of mechanical behavior that passes as the real thing.

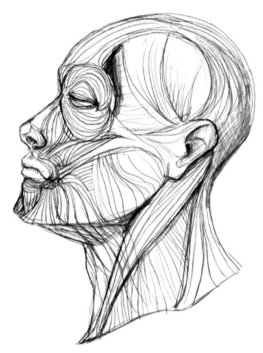

Facial muscles

Erick Miller facial expressions references

Maya software technology does make it possible, however, to achieve believability. The face has many unique challenges, and because of that, there is no one golden solution. Instead, each portion of the face must be analyzed and broken down to create a customized solution geared toward each unique problem.

Following are some portions and inherent topics that will be covered throughout this project.

Anatomy

Muscle based controls to achieve any expression or phoneme.

Mouth

Open mouth with volume and full range of realistic motion.

Lips

Fleshy and squashy lips, rolling lips and sticky lips.

Eyes

Lids, blinks, fleshy eye skin, dilation and iris refraction.

Skin

Pores, fine wrinkles and sub-surface scattering tricks.

Model deformation integrity

How the surface of the facial model is built is probably the single most important aspect of the rigging process. This is true for character setup in general, but is particularly critical for facial setups.

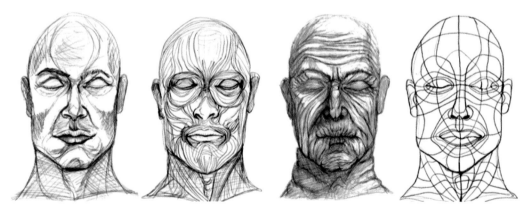

Facial muscles and skin wrinkles lead to good topology

Examine the above illustration from left to right. The image to the left is a simple face illustrating basic shadow planes. The second image from the left shows the muscle structure under the skin. Then comes an example of the wrinkle lines of the face. Lastly, the image to the right shows the primary basic edge flow that your model can have based on the intersection between muscle lines and wrinkle lines. It is very important to notice that the fiber direction of muscles in the face run perpendicular and traverse to the direction of the wrinkle lines. Combining these two directions into your final polygon model is the goal.

First off, for modern facial rigging, a single mesh quad polygon control cage optionally rendered as subdivision surfaces is the recommended way to go. The model must also have a really good wrinkle-line based edge flow, with radial circular edge loops radiating from the eyes, mouth, nose holes and ears.

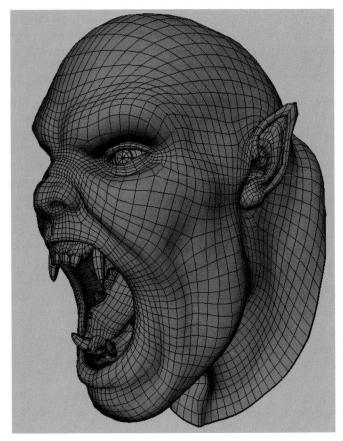

Ideal facial topology following muscle and wrinkle lines

You must also ensure that the model has plenty of resolution to support the most complex range of base expressions. If you are not sure about this, a good rule is to model the face into a broad smile, a wide-mouthed intense scream, or a stretched open-mouthed surprised face. Often, the need arises to add a few extra rows of edges to the model at primary creasing points, primarily in the laugh line, upper nose, forehead and brow wrinkle lines, as well as the wrinkle area around the eyes, and possibly the area under the lower lip and above the chin where frown lines occur. These are all hot spots to look for sufficient resolution, and as you begin rigging your character, demanding extra resolution in those areas can sometimes make or break the ability to achieve the correct necessary range of facial poses.

Conclusion

In this lesson, you learned about facial behavior, its underlying structure and the challenges that arise when rigging a face in a computer. You also learned the roots of creating good facial topology based on muscle and wrinkle lines, which is the key to good facial deformation.

In the next lesson, you will explore two different ways of rigging a face: blend shapes and joints.

Lesson 12 *Preparation*

This lesson explores the different ways of approaching facial rigging. You will see how to mix a joint driven setup with both blend shapes and clusters. Combining these techniques can greatly improve your facial animation since they increase the level of realism of your character's face.

Some of the beast's facial shapes

In this lesson you will learn the following:

- Reasons for using joints for facial rigging;

- Reasons for using blend shapes;

- How blend shapes work;

- Which shapes to create;

- Corrective blend shapes;

- How to set-up cluster controls.

Using joints for facial rigging

Deciding when to use hierarchies of joints and when to use modeled shapes to deform the face is pretty simple. Joints should be used for portions of the face that need to either rotate, or have some sort of driven transformation controls that are easier achieved using joints. Modeled shapes should be used for all other portions.

With this motivation, joints can be used to solve several facial rigging challenges. The most obvious one would be the jaw, which is a skeletal structure in real life that rotates and translates in an arcing manner.

Portions of the face that can be rigged using joint hierarchies are:

- Jaw;

- Rolling lips;

- Fleshy eyelids;

- Ears.

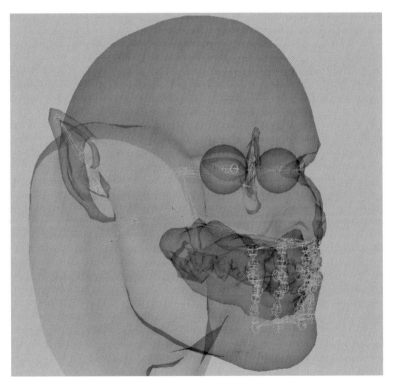

Joint setup used to deform the jaw, the ears, the lips and the eyelids

Using blend shapes for facial rigging

The reason for not using modeled shapes to open the jaw is because blend shapes are linearly interpolated. This means that the vertex follows a straight line as you blend in a model, so there is never an arc occurring when dealing with blend shapes. This is problematic when an arc is required or a more realistic motion path is needed for that expression. The face is naturally arced along the skull, so, unfortunately, this is one issue that can have a way of coming up more often than one would like.

On the other hand, blend shapes are really great deformers, and are probably one of the most useful and widely used nodes for facial rigging, so they should be considered and understood. The problem of arcs can be alleviated by doing *in-between* shapes, which cause the vertex to flow linearly between many shapes, giving the illusion of an arc movement.

It is also possible for an animator to creatively mix blend shapes together in an intuitive and influential way. The blend shape deformer is so powerful because it is stable and linear, and what you see is what you get. These qualities are absolutely invaluable when it comes to character deformations.

Mixed blend shapes resulting in different expressions on a single model

How blend shapes work

A blend shape is really a very simple, but powerful linear deformer. The way that a blend shape works is first it subtracts the original model points from your newly modeled shape, leaving only the difference values for each point.

Δ = Porig - Pshape

It then simply multiplies these differences with the blend shape's weight value for that shape. Next, it adds the result back with the original vertex point. For each point on the model, calculate the resulting deformed position P as follows:

$$P = ((\Delta a * Wa) + (\Delta b * Wb) + (\Delta c * Wc)) + Porig$$

Where Δa, Δb and Δc are the difference vectors coming from blend shapes, Wa, Wb and Wc are each blend shapes' weight value, and $Porig$ is the original input point prior to receiving the deformation.

> **Note:** When pushing the blend shape's weight value outside the 0 to 1 boundary, the difference vectors are still multiplied, resulting in overshooting of the shape's deformation.

Creating blend shapes

The anatomic nature of the face will be carefully considered when deciding what the target shapes for using blend shapes will be. Probably the single most important factor in creating the modeled shape based portion of the facial rig is using a combination of two very important methodologies.

1   Muscle based shapes

Create shapes based on the contraction, pulling and expansion of the face resulting from the activation of major muscle groups. These should be modeled first, deforming the geometry overall if needed.

2   Symmetry Upper/Lower Left/Middle/Right shapes

Create shapes based on splitting up the muscle based shapes into separate blend shapes that can be blended in as separate sliders. These shapes will give the ultimate asymmetrical shaping.

> **Note:** All of these shapes are used as blend shapes, giving coarse levels of control as well as finer levels of control.

At this point, there are no spoken phonemes or emotional mood based shapes. All the models will be solely motivated by the fact that they are uniquely caused by a separate group of facial muscles that push or pull mostly independently to create the modeled shape. The models will all be created without any jaw opening, and if the jaw must be opened to get a good-looking shape, it should be subtracted back out from the shape before the model is finished and applied as one of the blend shapes. This way all the multiple shapes can be more easily combined together, in order to create any phoneme, emotion, or possible facial pose.

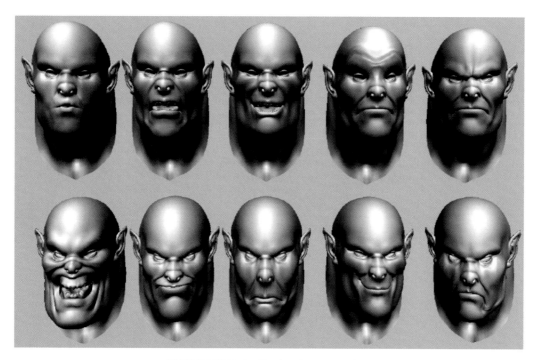

Muscle based shapes without any jaw movements

The above image shows a few facial muscle based targets that were modeled with the muscle based group methodology in mind. Notice that many of the shapes can be pushed to extreme poses for a wider range of control without the model tearing or cracking. It is also important to note that although models attempt to isolate muscle groups, the fact that skin pulls with a falloff into other regions of the face should definitely be considered. Examples of this are the push and pull of the skin in the cheeks and chin when moving the lip muscles, and the push and pull of the skin on the top of the head and ears when moving the forehead muscles.

Movie: *See the movie mixingBlendshapes.avi in the support files for a general idea of how easily shapes can be mixed together.*

Following is a fairly extensive list of muscle based facial targets that can be modeled as a starting point for a broad range of facial expression capabilities (when properly symmetrically separated and then re-combined during animation):

- Brow down/up (furrow and raise);

- Forehead brow sideways (inward pull/outward stretch);

- Eye blinks (to be covered in Lesson 14);

- Wide-open eyes;

- Tightly closed/squinted eyes;

- Nose inward, outward and downward flares;

- Nose sneer/snarl;

- Squinted upper cheeks/lower eyes (including crows feet);

- Puffed out and sucked in cheeks;

- Lips up/down (upward and downward facial shrugs);

- Lip corners up/down (pull of smile, push of frown);

- Lip corners sideways (inward pull/outward stretch);

- Vertically flattened/tightened lips and puffed out lips;

- Open mouthed smile;

- Ooo mouth shapes (several in-between targets required);

- Squeezed close tightened lips (closed lip purse/pucker);

- Upward lip sneer/snarl & downward lip sneer;

- Jaw clench/forehead clench/neck clench.

Once the required shapes are modeled, they need to be carefully separated into individual facial areas. Doing so gives you control of facial areas that are clearly capable of asymmetric changes.

You can analytically split the face up into upper, middle and lower as well as left, middle and right regions. Each one of the muscle based shapes should then be split up into these separate regions carefully using the Edit Membership Tool on a blend shaped model, and then tweaking each shape so that it has a smooth fall-off around the edges of each region.

> **Tip:** Be sure to check out the Condensed Reference Video Appendix contained on the Hyper-Real Facial Setup DVD, which has high quality video footage of real human facial movement based on the above outlined muscle based shapes.

The following image clearly shows the separate regions that may move independently in a face separated into symmetrical regions, where each shape should be roughly split up based on the region of the grid in which it falls. The red grid is the primary priority grid, and the light blue lines are secondary priority regions that give much finer grain separation, but often are overkill. For example, the separation of any single brow shape could range in size anywhere between 1 to 9 separate brow shapes: one for the whole, one for the left and right, and one for each individual split section. Note that this fine level of distinction is usually not needed for the majority of shapes, but is often requested by the animator when a certain pose becomes un-achievable without it.

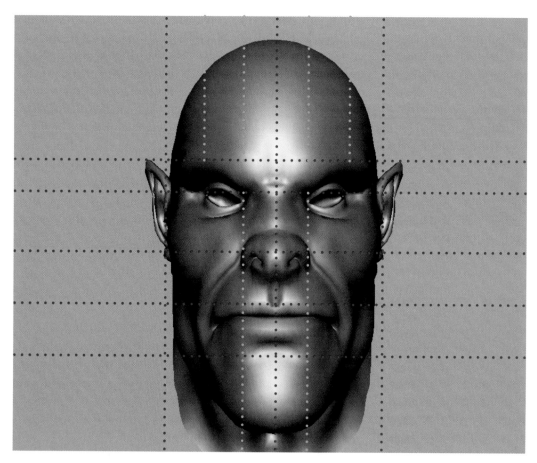

The different facial regions

Tip: It is a good idea to wait for specific requests before attempting to generate fine level shapes. Sticking with the red grid is usually quite a lot to start testing with anyhow.

Corrective shapes

Modeling corrective shapes to fix deformation when joints deform the face is the perfect techniques combination to achieve the exact pose you are attempting to reach. To do so, the corrective blend shape needs to be animated using a Set Driven Key that is activated when the joints rotate.

Probably the most obvious and expected corrective blend shape is one driven by the jaw's rotation, which will allow the mouth's natural O shape to appear and stretch in a visually appropriate way, as though it is skin that is maintaining some sort of volume around the structure of the jaw and skull as the mouth opens. Other corrective shapes will be used as examples to get the rolling lip shaped a little quicker.

Note: *You will see in the next lesson how to create and set-up a corrective blend shape for the mouth to use with the jaw.*

Clusters

The final setup involves one more set of controls. These are the cluster based shape controls. These will be covered in more detail later, but it is important to note what they are and why they can and probably should be used. Clusters are very similar to joints, except they have some nice transformation capabilities that give them a bit more power when it comes to the particular challenge of regionally based facial controls. First off, they can be used and rigged up in such a way that controllers for the clusters stay attached to the mesh while it deforms. This is really useful because all the deformation techniques that are being layered together would otherwise cause cluster controls to float in the wrong place for regions of the face that had already been animated with blend shapes.

The following diagram shows circled regions of the face where smoothly weighted cluster based facial controls can be applied.

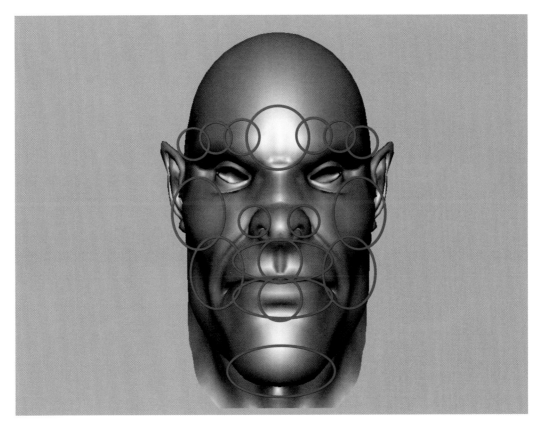

Possible cluster regions

Finally, you must understand that these controls are solely meant to give the animator sculptural control over the face, but in a smoothly weighted way. These clusters are not meant to crease wrinkle lines very much, and should smoothly drop off to zero around their edges. This way the muscle based shapes will be used for the bulk of the realistic-looking posing and the shaping can be used to add some rotational offsets, or to slide the pose over a little bit. These clusters are in no way meant to replace the blend shape controls, and should be thought of as a valuable secondary set of facial controls.

Testing the facial setup

Once you have all the blend shapes, joints and cluster controls set-up and everything is running well, you must put the rig through an extensive animation test where it is ideally tested by multiple animators. This test should have the character speak all the possible phonemes, as well as going through a full range of emotional shifts combined with dialogue. The combination of individually moving muscle based motion should begin to make more sense as you see the control it gives animators to realistically time and shape independent facial movements as well as add subtle asymmetrical details.

> **Note:** Watch the movie testAnimation.avi from the support file to see a simple test made with the beast's setup.

Extra work and concepts

Sometimes shapes will not behave exactly as expected. This can be the case particularly with shapes that move different muscles and vertices in the same general direction, but at differing rates. Unexpected and unappealing double transformations that cause ripping can occur. You will cover some topics on how to deal with double transformations using driven multipliers as a rigging topic later on, but first these problems should be addressed in the modeled shapes as much as possible. Splitting certain shapes out that don't coincide directly with a muscle group, but help create a very specific form in the face is sometimes necessary. Think of what you would need to do if you had to make a super slow motion scene of a face getting punched so hard that it broke the skin and fractured part of the skull beneath, or perhaps a slow motion close-up of a suicidal gunshot from within the mouth. Although these are quite gruesome examples, this sort of thing gets done quite often in visual effects, because it cannot be done with the real actor. These types of cases definitely require custom shape models or additional controls to get the job done.

Additional blend shapes, not purely muscle based, are what you could call signature poses. This is the case with many famous celebrities; they have certain key facial expressions or looks that they are well known for, which have helped make them famous and often define their personae. Capturing this look is incredibly important, and if necessary, justifies an entirely new set of models just to achieve the signature poses. It is usually possible to get really close with the rig and then just duplicate off the model and do the subtle tweaks until it looks correct. This pose can then be used to blend in at varying degrees to make the face look more in character.

Asymmetrical additive drooping shapes that include well-formed wrinkle lines can also be quite useful depending on the need of the character. What this means is that you make a few blend shapes that simply droop parts of the face very subtly, as though the skin is being slightly pulled up and pushed around by a force such as gravity or by your finger. These sorts of shapes are pretty easy to generate and they can be used generically in many circumstances. For example, they can be very useful for an animator to make the face skin look more dynamic during a quick whipping the head around or a forceful motion, and general subtle drooping can help to add a look of tiredness or depravity to any facial expression.

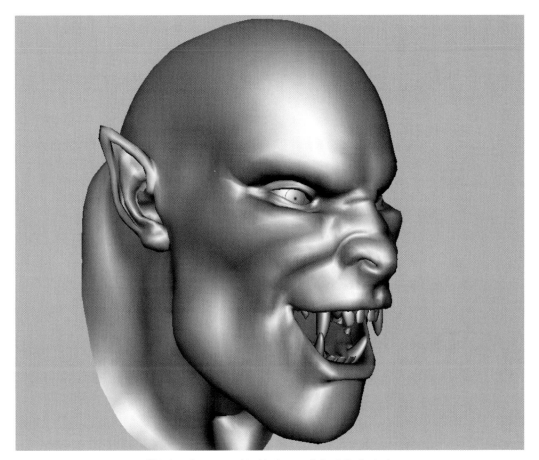

Signature shapes can add a lot when creating a distinctive look

Conclusion

As you have seen throughout this lesson, creating a facial setup usually requires lots of planning. You must take into consideration what you need the character to do, what specialties it requires and how much effort and level of control you should put into the facial rig. All three techniques, joints, blend shapes and clusters, should be used together in a character that requires as much definition as the beast example, but it is up to you to ascertain the combination of techniques.

In the next lesson, you will implement a jaw bone to the beast along with corrective blend shapes.

Lesson 13 *The jaw*

Now that the specific muscle structural details, challenges and difficulties, as well as explanations for the motivations and techniques has been laid out, the next lessons will provide more detailed insight into the specific rigging techniques used to create these facial rigging and deformation effects.

In this lesson, you will add a jaw bone to the beast, and then add a corrective blend shape setup with driven keys to make it move in a realistic manner.

In this lesson you will learn the following:

- How to create a jaw setup;

- How to adjust the skinning of the head;

- How to create a corrective blend shape;

- How to automate the blend shape to the jaw.

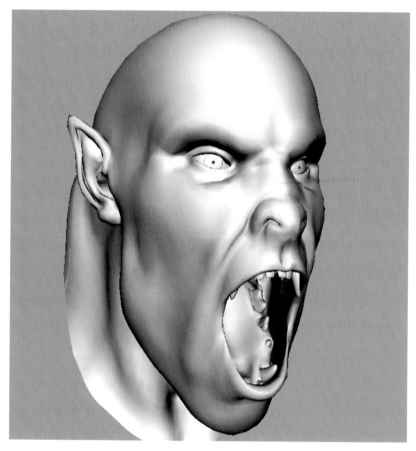

The mouth's extreme pose

Head joints

In this exercise you will create a head setup that will allow you to animate the jaw and the head independently from each other.

1 Scene file

- Open the scene file *13-jaw_01.ma*.

This scene contains the beast's head along with the neck joints and a few selection sets.

2 Create the lower jaw

- Select **Skeleton** → **Joint Tool.**

- From the *side* view, click on the *headJA_1* bone.

Doing so tells the Joint Tool that you want to create a joint chain starting from the head joint.

- **Create** a joint as the jaw pivot.

The pivot of the jaw almost always exists in a clearly defined area just below the ear, along a line that runs perpendicular to another line that you could draw from the earlobe to the corner of the eye; it is never behind the ear or as far forward as the cheek. Sometimes it is worth experimenting with the pivot location in order to discover what the best location for the jaw is, based on the complexity of your model or its derivation from a human being.

- **Create** another joint at the chin location.

- **Rename** the first joint *jawLowerJA_1* and the end joint *jawLowerJEnd_1*.

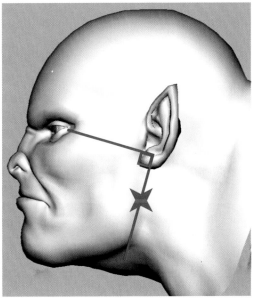

The jaw pivot estimated location

3 Create the upper jaw

You will now add two more joints to create the upper jaw hierarchy.

- Select **Skeleton** → **Joint Tool.**

- From the *side* view, click on the *headJA_1* bone.

- Hold down the **v** key and snap a new joint to the *jawLowerJA_1*.

Doing so will create the upper jaw hierarchy with the exact same pivot as the lower jaw hierarchy.

- **Create** another joint in the area behind the nose.

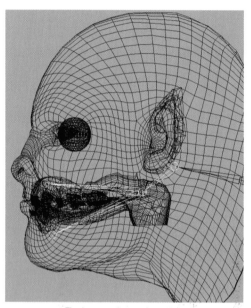

The lower and upper jaw setup

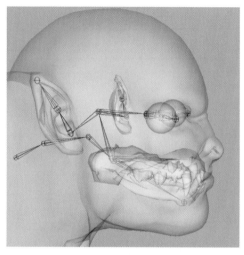

The entire head joint setup

- **Rename** the first joint *jawUpperJA_1* and the end joint *jawUpperJEnd_1*.

4 Other head joints

At this point, you might want to create more joints to control others parts of the face, such as the eyes and ears.

> **Note:** *The eye setup will be covered in the next lesson.*

Skinning the head

The main skeletal hierarchy for weighting the jaw can consist of two joints, both having pivots in the exact same location at the jaw, and both being children of the same parent, at the main head joint. This allows you to rotate the head upwards from the same single pivot and not change the jaw location, as well as conventionally rotate the jaw.

1 Bind the head

- **Select** the neck joints, the jawLowerJA_1 and jawUpperJA_1 joints, and then Shift-select the head geometry.

- Select **Skin** → **Bind Skin** → **Smooth Bind.**

2 Binding the teeth

- **Smooth bind** the teeth to their respective jaw bones.

Binding the teeth rather than parenting them to the joints will allow you to keep the geometry outside the joint hierarchy.

3 Selection sets

By using selection sets, you can quickly set the weight assignment of the geometry and then begin to refine the influence maps.

- Open the Outliner.

- **RMB-click** on the *lowerJaw* selection set and then select **Select Set Members.**

The vertices that were previously assigned to this set are now selected.

- Select **Skin** → **Edit Smooth Skin** → **Paint Skin Weights Tool.**

- In the tool window, highlight *jawLowerJA_1,* then select **Replace** with a value of **1.0**.

- Click the **Flood** button.

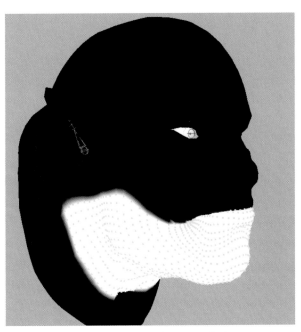

Flooding the vertices in the current selection

Doing so will set the weight of the selected vertices to be fully assigned to the currently highlighted influence.

- **Repeat** the previous steps for the *upperJaw* and *neck* selection sets.

4   Skinning

Carefully and patiently painting well distributed weights for the joint that opens the mouth is probably the single most important first step to creating a believable facial deformation rig. Concentrate on a nice falloff radiating from the corners of the lips, wrapping lightly upwards toward the temple and laugh-lines, and downward towards the chin.

To increase the quality of the deformation, add subtle amounts of weighting to the jaw into areas like the lower nose and the upper lip. You should also add some subtle weight values from the chin just below the lower lip onto the upper portion of the head to increase subtle movement of the skin. These little details are an important part of creating a mouth that appears realistically fleshy when the jaw opens. It will give the upper and lower regions above the lips an understated impression of being pulled by muscle and stretched.

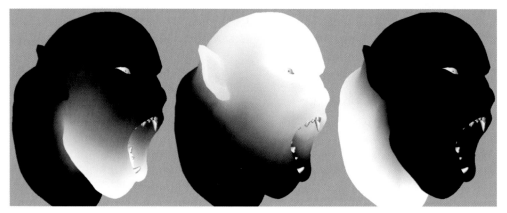

The jaw, head and neck influences

5   Save your work

6   Completed scene file

- Open the scene file *13-jaw_02.ma* from the support files.

- **Rotate** the upper and lower jaw bone to see the effect of the weighting over the entire head.

Notice the smooth and subtle fall-off between the weights, which causes a nice averaged stretching of the entire facial skin and gives a fleshy appearance when the jaw is open. This will be the only mechanism for opening the character's jaw, which will get layered in with the muscle and symmetry based blend shape controls, as well as the regionally based cluster controls.

> **Note:** See the movie jawRangeOfMotion.avi for an example of the wide range that the final jaw
> setup can animate.

Corrective blend shape

The corrective blend shape will allow the mouth to stretch to maintain volume. It is easy to create by
simply duplicating the un-deformed base model and making a front of chain blend shape.

1 Scene file

- Continue with your own scene.

Or

- Open the scene file *13-jaw_02.ma*.

2 Duplicate the head

- **Duplicate** the head geometry without any deformations.

> **Tip:** To make sure the head is not deformed by the skinCluster, highlight it in the Channel Box
> and set the Envelope attribute to 0 (Off) for when you duplicate the geometry.

- **Move** the head aside.
- **Rename** the duplicated geometry to *OpenMouthCorrective*.

3 Create the blend shape

Even if the shapes are currently identical, you will create the blend shape deformer right away. This
will allow you to see the effect of the immediate deformations on the original head.

- Select the *OpenMouthCorrective* shape, then **Shift-select** the original head.
- Select **Deform** → **Create Blend Shape** → ❑.
- In the option window, under the Advance tab, set Deformation Order to Front Of Chain.

> **Note:** The Front Of Chain deformation order will insert the blend shape before any other deformers,
> thus having the deformation applied on the original geometry.

- Click the Create button.

4 Set Driven Keys

You must now set separate driven keys on both the lower and upper jaw.

- When the lower jaw is in its default position, the corrective blend shape should be set at **0**, and when it rotates down to its most extreme pose, it should increase to **1**.

- **Repeat** the previous step, but for the upper jaw rotating up.

5 Deform the corrective shape

- **Rotate** down the jaw to its most extreme pose.

- Select the *OpenMouthCorrective* shape and select **Deform** → **Create Lattice**.

- Set the resolution of the lattice so that you get enough resolution to tweak the mouth area as follows:

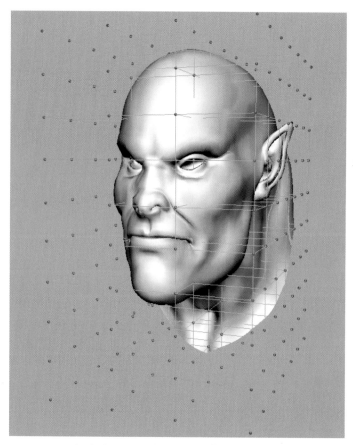

Lattice box used to deform the corrective head

- **Deform** the lattice so that the lip volume looks narrower on the original head when the mouth is open.

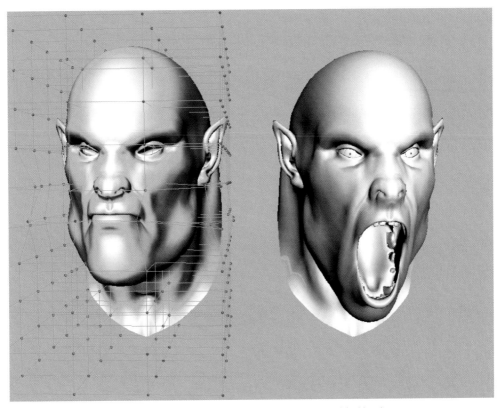

The deformed corrective blend shape and its effect on the original head

6 Test the animation

- **Rotate** the lower and upper jaw to see the effect of the corrective blend shape.

- **Tweak** the lattice as needed.

7 Save your work

- Save your work as *13-jaw_03.ma*.

Conclusion

In this lesson, you experimented with a jaw setup with two joints to control the lower and upper portion of the head independently. You also learned a useful way to create corrective blend shapes, which will dramatically increase the level of realism of your character.

In the next lesson, you will learn how to set up fleshy eyes and eye blinks.

Lesson 14 *The eyes*

The eyes of a character are arguably the most emotive part of the face and they must be carefully set-up in order to achieve hyper-realism. You will now be shown techniques to rig the eyes so that they look as dynamic and fleshy as human eyes. Doing so involves eye blinks, eyelid deformation and pupil dilatation.

In this lesson you will learn the following:

- Eye blink shapes;

- How to create a fleshy eye setup;

- Mixing deformers and blend shapes;

- About pupil dilatation.

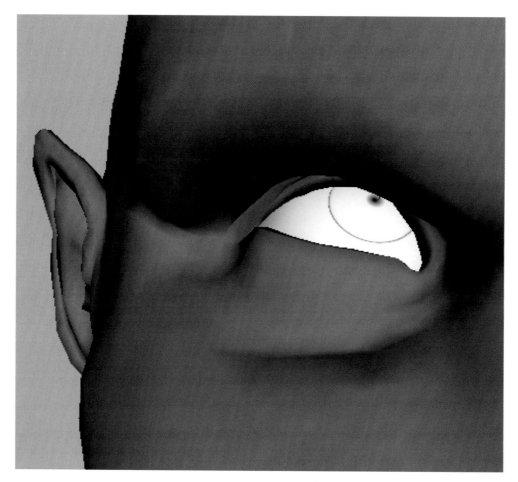

The final effect

Eye blinks

Eye blinks are actually a straightforward set of shapes. In this example, you will model the eye blink shapes as a whole, but note that you could also model them split into upper and lower shapes.

Following are a few shapes that should be carefully modeled for the lids.

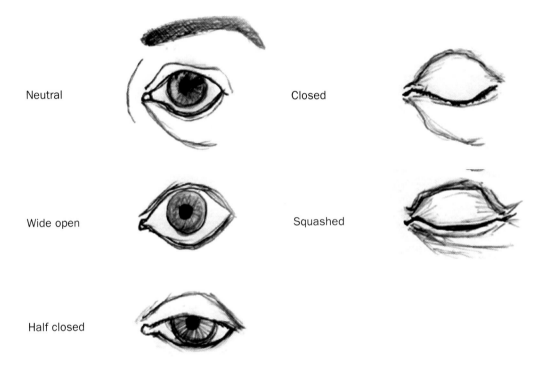

Neutral

Closed

Wide open

Squashed

Half closed

Eye shapes to be modeled

> **Note:** The wide open shape is not part of the eye blink, but it is still a very important shape to have.

The following demonstrates how to create the appropriate blend shape deformer to blink the eyes.

> **Note:** For simplicity reasons, this exercise covers only the rigging of the right eye of the beast. For the left eye, simply duplicate the steps.

1   Scene file

- Open the scene file *14-eyes_01.ma*.

This scene contains the beast's head and eyes.

2   Modeling the shapes

- **Duplicate** the beast's head with the eyes **three times**.

> **Tip:**   *It is important to duplicate the head with the eyes because you need them to properly model the eyelids closing.*

- **Move** the duplicates aside to the original head.
- **Model** the *half closed*, *closed* and *squashed* shapes required for the right eye blink.

 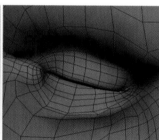 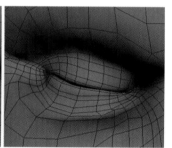

The half closed, closed and squashed eyelid shapes

> **Note:**   *Notice the last two blink shapes are subtly different. The last one has compressed skin around the lids, attempting to create the effect of compression as the skin touches together during a blink.*

3   Blend shapes with in-between

In-between blend shapes place the desired shapes in series within the same blend shape attribute.

- Select the three blend shapes in the order you want them to be in the blend shape series.

- **Shift-select** the original beast head.

- Select **Deform** → **Create Blend Shape** → ☐.

- Make sure to turn On the In-Between option, then click the Create button.

4   Test the results

When you change the blend shape deformer's attribute, you should see the eye blinking, going through three blink shapes and causing the eye to appear more realistic as it closes.

Note: *Watch the movie eyeBlink.avi to see an animated version of the blend shapes.*

5   Save your work

- Save your work as *14-eyes_02.ma*.

Fleshy eyes

The fleshy eyes are an important part of the facial setup, because they add a necessary level of realism. Basically, the setup will have the eyelids moving and following the eyes as they look up and down, just as eyes do naturally.

There are several ways to rig fleshy eyes, and some are more complete than others. The technique described here details a combination of skinning, Set Driven Keys, vector utility nodes and sculpt deformers.

Binding the head and eyes

1   Scene file

- Open the scene file *14-fleshyEyes_01.ma*.

This scene contains the beast's head, along with several pre-modeled shapes that will be covered later in this exercise.

2 Eye joints

- Use the **Joint Tool** to draw joints as follows:

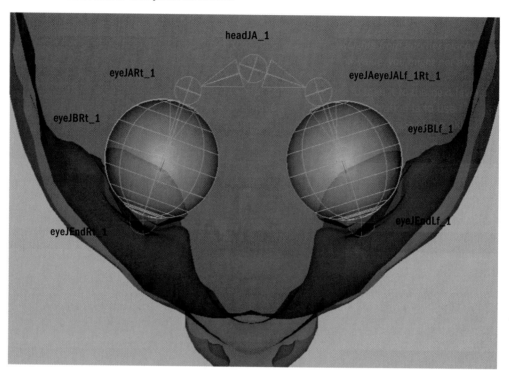

The head joints for the purpose of this example

You absolutely need a joint for each eye that has the same pivot as the center of the eyeball. This joint's rotation axis should also be aligned with the plane of the eye and the eye socket.

Tip: *You can use the same constraint technique shown in Lesson 7 to snap the eye joints in the center of the eye geometry.*

- **Rename** the joints properly.

3 Skinning

- **Smooth bind** the eye to its respective eye joint.
- **Smooth bind** the head to the two eye joints and *headJA_1*.

The eye joints should be subtly weighted onto the area around the eyes and eyelids. The weighting value onto these joints should not be very high. Consider using values like **0.2** *and smooth flooding a few times with the Paint Skin Weights Tool to achieve a nice and smooth fade-off.*

Notice the low influence of the eye joint on the eyelids

4   **Save your work**

- Save your scene as *14-fleshyEyes_02.ma*.

Blend shapes

The scene you have been using thus far also contains several shapes added to the shapes of the previous example, in order to achieve the full fleshy eye effect.

The following four images are the upper lid and lower lid extreme open and closed shapes. These shapes will be used in conjunction with the eye joint in order to control the eyelid deformation when the character is looking up or down.

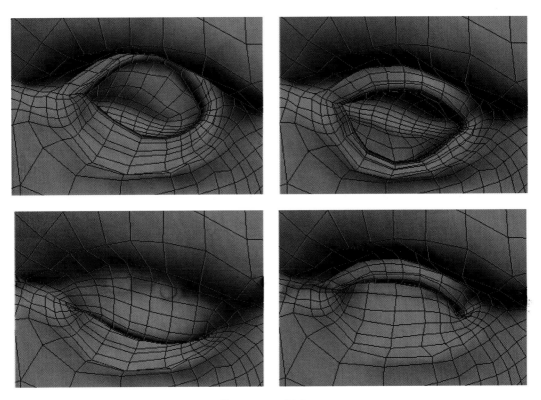

The extreme eyelid shapes

The following six images will be used to achieve the bump look of the skin as the eyeball moves around under the eyelid.

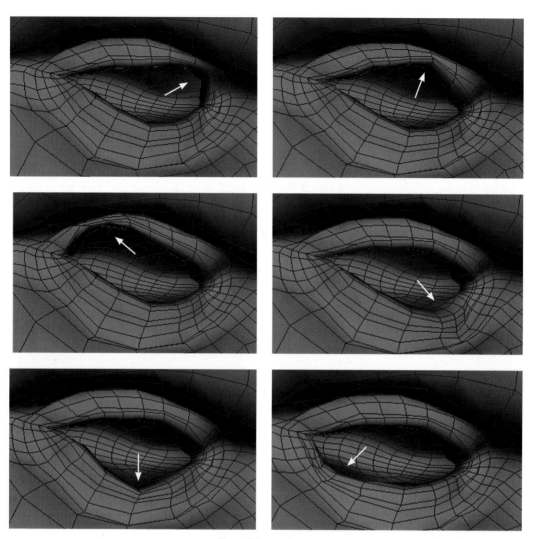

The eyelid bump shapes

1   Scene file

- Continue with the scene from the last example.

2   Blend shapes

- Create a **Front Of Chain Blend Shape** with all the shapes on the original skinned head.

> **Tip:**   *Don't forget to turn Off the In-Between option in the blend shape window.*

- **Rename** the blend shape node *fleshyEyes*.

3   Set Driven Keys

You will now have to create Set Driven Keys based on the upward motion of the eyeball. When the eye is moving up, you want both the upper and lower eyelids to move up as well to keep the natural shape of the eye. Repeat the same thing as the eyeball moves downward.

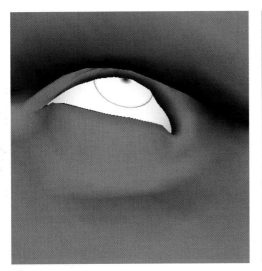

The up and down motion of the eye

Bump eyelid

At this point, you have a decent looking fleshy eye. You could stop here if you don't require further detail, but the following example will implement a bump eyelid to the setup.

The idea here is to determine which of the bump eyelid shapes to use as the eye is looking around. To do so, you will use a combination of subtraction utility nodes piped into a dot product, taking into account the closest UV position on a NURBS circle.

1   Circle

- **Create** a NURBS circle.

- **Position** and **shape** the circle to roughly fit the eye socket, where the skull would be.

- **Rename** the circle to *eye_socket_curve*.

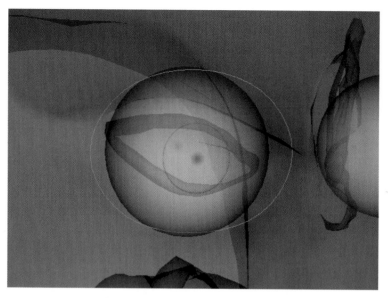

The circle shaped to fit the skull's eye socket

2 Locators

- **Create** three locators.

- **Rename** the locators *eye_tip_pt*, *eye_pt* and *eye_plane_pt*.

- **Point constrain** the locators to each of the three eye joints as follows:

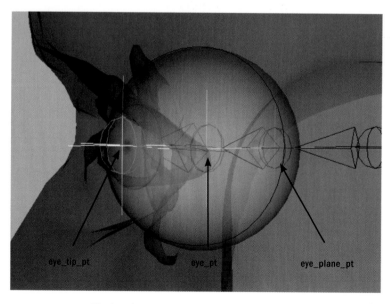

The three locators point constrained to the eye joints

Note: *Do not freeze the transformations on the locators. You will be using their translation in the next step.*

3 Translation vectors

- Open the **Window** → **Rendering Editors** → **Hypershade**.

- With the three locators selected, click on the **Input and Output Connections** button.

- Select **Create** → **General Utilities** → **Plus Minus Average**.

- Click on the output arrow of the *eye_plane_pt* node and select the *translate* attribute, then plug it into the *input3D[0]* attribute on the *plusMinusAverage1* node.

- **Repeat** the step above to plug the *eye_pt.translate* attribute into the *input3D[1]* of the *plusMinusAverage1* node.

- **Create** another **Plus Minus Average** node.

- **Plug** the *eye_tip_pt.translate* to the *plusMinusAverage2.input3D[0]*.

- **Plug** the *eye_pt.translate* to the *plusMinusAverage2.input3D[1]*.

- Set both *plusMinusAverage* nodes' **Operation** to **Subtract**.

Doing so will give you two translation vectors that can be used in a dot product to get a number between zero and one to use with the blend shape deformer.

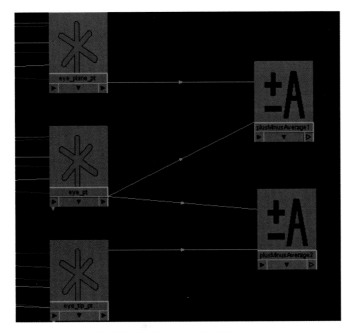

The locators connected to the utility nodes

4 Vector product

- Select **Create** → **General Utilities** → **Vector Product**.

- **Connect** the output of both *plusMinusAverage* nodes into the **input1** and **input2** of the *vectorProduct1* node.

- **Add** a custom attribute called *dotProduct* on the *eye_socket_curve*.

- **Connect** the *ouputX* of the *vectorProduct1* to this new *dotProduct* attribute.

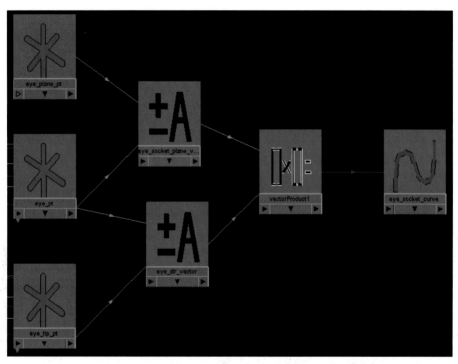

The vector product connected to the custom attribute on the socket curve

5 Closest point on surface

Before you can use the dot product, you need to find something to reliably drive the blend shapes of the fleshy eyes using simple Set Driven Keys. Since the eye is restricted to rotate only on two axes, the closest UV value of a NURBS surface with the shape of the eye will work perfectly.

- **Create** a circle.

- Hold down **c** then **click+drag** to snap the circle to the *eye_socket_curve*.

- **Scale** the circle down and **rotate** it so it is perpendicular to the *eye_socket_curve*.

- Select the small circle, then **Shift-select** the *eye_socket_curve*.

- Select **Surfaces** → **Extrude**.

- **Type** the following in the Command Line to create a *closestPointOnSurface* node:

  createNode closestPointOnSurface;

- **Connect** the *worldSpace[0]* attribute of the NURBS surface's shape to the *closestPointOnSurface*'s *inputSurface*.

- **Connect** *eye_tip_pt.translate* to *closestPointOnSurface.inPosition*.

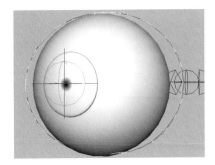

The simple NURBS surface created by doing a loft

This setup calculates the closest point on the surface from the tip of the eyeball when it rotates around. This is a useful technique because it is angle independent, and outputs a single value that interpolates properly and can directly represent the blend shape target that the eyeball should be driven to.

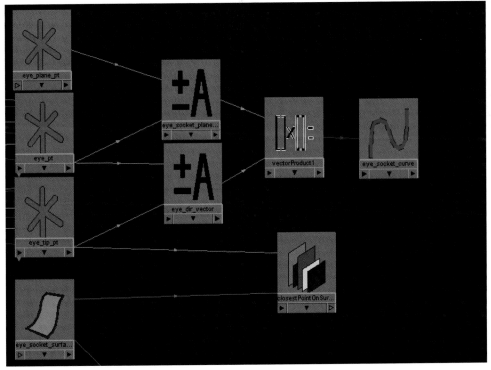

The closest point on surface's connections

- **Add** a custom attribute called *PARAM* to the NURBS surface.

- **Connect** *closestPointOnSurface. parameterU* to the NURBS surface's *PARAM* attribute.

6 Set Driven Keys

Now, move the eyeball around with the eye joint, but use Set Driven Keys to drive the different blend shape values depending on the PARAM value of the NURBS surface.

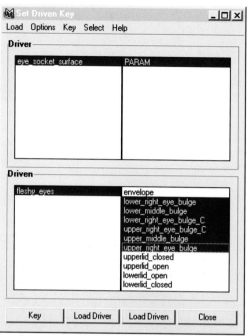

The Set Driven Key window

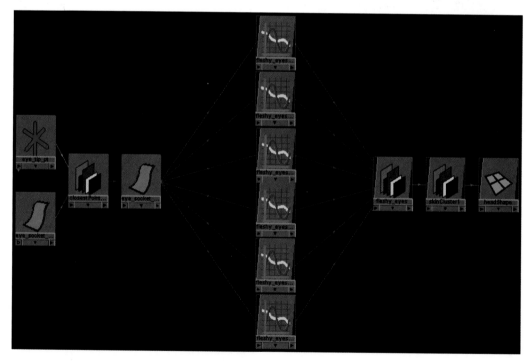

The driven keys network

7 Multipliers

Next, you need to insert multiplier utility nodes between the Set Driven Keys and the blend shape attributes based on another Set Driven Key that uses the dot product between the eye vector and the original opposite eye vector as its driver to determine the multiplier. The dot product automatically gives us a gradient between zero and one, but you will use a Set Driven Key to further tweak this gradient value so that it gives you the exact fleshy eye look you want.

- Select **Create** → **General Utilities** → **Multiply Divide**.

- **Insert** the *multiplierDivide* node between the connection of the Set Driven Key output and the blend shape input.

- **Repeat** in order to insert other *multiplyDivide* nodes for the remaining Set Driven Key animation nodes.

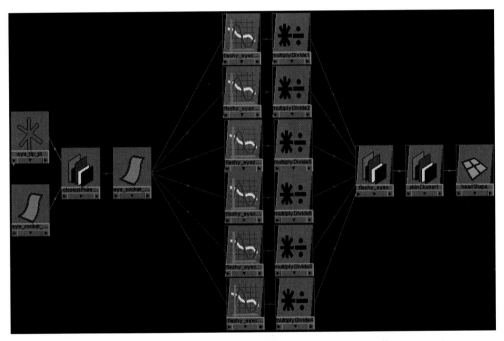

The inserted multiplyDivide nodes

8 Finalize the bump setup

- Hook another single *multiplyDivide* node into the ones you just created in the previous step.

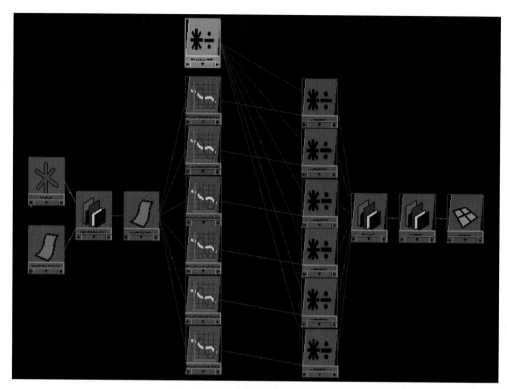

The last multiplyDivide node in the setup

- Create a final Set Driven Key by rotating the eye joint, using the *dotProduct* custom attribute on the *eye_socket_curve* as the driver and the last *multiplyDivide* node as the driven.

Tip: *In order for the final effect to be animatable along with the head, you must parent eye_socket_curve to the head. If you deleted the history on the NURBS surface, you must also parent it or bind it to the head.*

Sculpt deformers

Additional semi-dynamic looking sliding and bulging of the eye can be added with sculpt deformers. You need one sculpt deformer for the round section of the eyeball, and another one for the bulged portion that surrounds the iris of the outer eyeball.

- Select the head geometry, then select **Deform → Create Sculpt Deformer** twice to create two sculpt deformers.

- **Parent** the deformer's locators to their respective sculpt deformers.

- **Place** and **scale** them as follows:

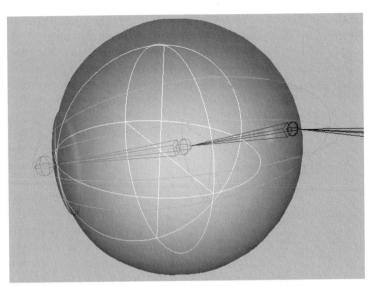

The sculpt deformers used to deform the eyelid dynamically

- **Parent** the sculpt deformers to the eyeball joint.

- **Tweak** the **Maximum Displacement** and **Dropoff Distance** attributes to your liking.

- **Reduce** the **Envelope** value of the sculpt nodes, so that their overall effect is multiplied just enough to look good when combined with the rest of the effect.

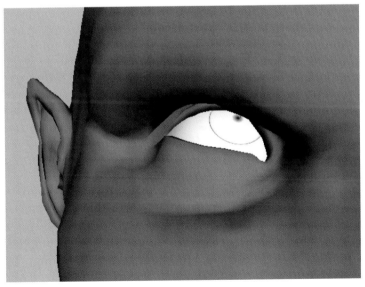

The final effect

9   Save your work

- Save your scene as *14-fleshyEyes_03.ma*.

> **Note:** *Check out the final effect of the fleshy eyes by viewing the movie fleshyEyes.avi.*

Pupil dilatation

The pupil dilatation can be done very simply, depending on the way the eye of your character is set-up and the quality of the effect you want to achieve. For instance, you can do it with a couple of blend shapes on the iris geometry.

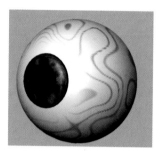

The iris dilatation done with blend shapes

> **Movie:** *Check out the movie file iris.avi.*

Basically, all that is needed to achieve this look is the creation of two modeled blend shapes on the eye geometry. The modeling should occur with a hardware shader attached to the geometry in high quality display mode, which allows the modeler to see how changing the model is warping the texture mapped area, which appears to cause pupil dilatation. The following shows the two eye shapes required for the iris dilatation:

- A fully dilated iris

A model that expands the center isoparms outward along the averaged plane of the iris, expanding and stretching out the UV coordinates on the area of the NURBS eyeball surface that the iris texture map will be attached to.

- A fully contracted iris

This would be a super beady-eyed model that appears as though there is almost no pupil at all.

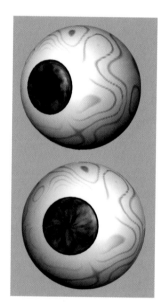

The iris shapes

Movie: *Open the scene file 14-irisDilatation.ma for an example.*

Conclusion

In this lesson, you created a custom fleshy eye setup. You experimented here with a complex deformer and utility node network, which allowed you to achieve the required deformation to properly set-up the eye rig. It is now up to you to extract from this lesson the techniques that you want to use for your character's facial setup.

In the next lesson, you will create custom facial controls.

Lesson 15 *Face controls*

In this lesson, you will create face controls attached to the skin surface. These controls will make usage of clusters on mesh, which are really handy to use as additional translation controls to move the mesh around. Face controls are special because they will stay stuck on the mesh's surface, even as it deforms through other deformers.

In this lesson you will learn the following:

- How to create surface dependent controls;

- How to create clusters;

- How to paint cluster influence.

Example of facial controls

Cluster on mesh

In order to create a control that follows the mesh surface however the surface moves, you need to create a small setup that will constrain the control to the mesh components. Since this is a task that might end up being repetitive, you will use a simple MEL script that automates the setup creation.

The *rivet.mel* script is quite ingenious because it internally creates a small NURBS patch across the two polygonal edges that you are constraining to, and then uses this NURBS surface to pull the required information needed to constrain the face control.

1 Scene file

- Open the scene file *15-clusterOnMesh_01.ma*.

This scene contains the skinned beast's head with blend shapes.

2 MEL script

- **Source** the MEL script called *rivet.mel* from the support files.

- Select two parallel polygonal edges like the following:

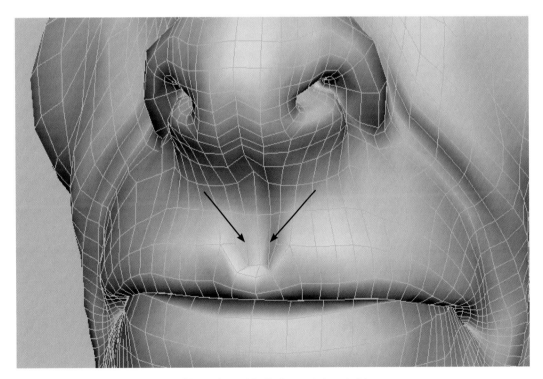

Edges to be used for the face control constraint

- **Execute** `rivet` in the Command Line.

Doing so, you will get a locator that is stuck at that location in position and orientation on the mesh.

3 Cluster

- From the Outliner, **highlight** the set named *upperLip*.

- **RMB-click** on the set and select **Select Set Members**.

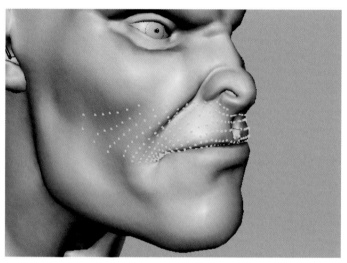

The vertices that are part of the upper lip set

- Select **Deform → Create Cluster**.

A cluster handle will appear and deform the selected vertices.

> **Note:** *Make sure the Relative option is turned On in the cluster's options.*

- Using the **Insert** key, snap the pivot of the cluster to the *rivet1* locator.

- With the *head* geometry selected, select **Deform → Paint Cluster Weights Tool → ❑**.

- Select the Smooth Paint Operation and then click the Flood button a couple of times.

Doing so will have the cluster's influence fall-off with a nice gradient.

- **Adjust** the cluster's weights as needed.

The upper lip's cluster influence

- **RMB-click** on the *head* geometry, then select **Inputs** → **All Inputs...**

- **MMB-click+drag** the cluster deformer below the head's skinCluster.

Doing so will reorganize the deformation order of the head's deformers so that the cluster is evaluated before the skin cluster.

Tip: *Depending on how you parent the cluster into your hierarchy, you might have to turn off the Inherits Transform options in the cluster's Attribute Editor.*

4   Orient constraint

Since the aim constraint created automatically with the rivet script could potentially cause Gimbal lock problems down the line, you will replace it with a simple orient constraint.

- **Delete** the aim constraint under the *rivet1* locator.

- **Zero out** the rotation values of the *rivet1* locator.

- Select the upper and lower joint used for animation, then **Shift-select** the *rivet1* locator.

- Select **Constrain** → **Orient** → ☐.

- Make sure to turn **Off** the **Maintain Offset** option, then click the **Add** button.

- Set the upper jaw joint's weight of the orient constraint to **0.9** and the lower jaw weight to **0.1**.

This will cause the orientation of the locator to mainly follow the upper jaw's rotations.

5 Face control

You must now create a controller object that you will use to pick and deform the upper lip. In this example, you will use a small NURBS sphere, but you could also use whatever else you would like, such as curves, polygons, locators, etc.

- **Create** a simple **NURBS sphere** and **place** it in front of the upper lip as follows:

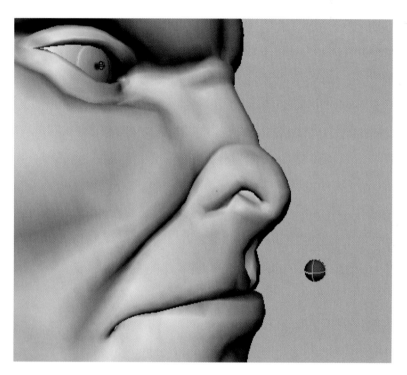

The NURBS sphere to be used as the control object

- Open the Attribute Editor for the NURBS sphere.

- Under the **Object Display** section, set **Enable Override** in the **Drawing Overrides** and then choose a **Color** of your liking.

- Through the Hypergraph, graph the connections to the sphere and break the connection between the surface and its shading group.

Doing so will cause the sphere to have no shading at all and be displayed opaquely.

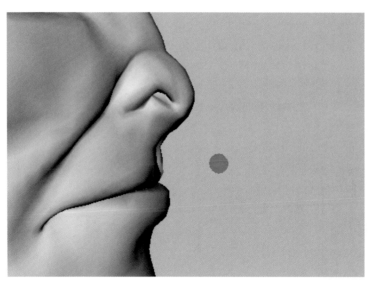

The colored sphere

- **Rename** the sphere as *upperLipControl*.

- **Freeze** the sphere's transformations.

- Press the **Insert** key, then snap the pivot of the sphere to the *rivet1* locator.

6   Hierarchy

- Press **Ctrl+g** three times.

Those groups will serve as animation overrides to the control sphere.

- **Parent** the top group to *rivet1*.

- **Freeze** the transformations of the groups.

- **Parent** the sphere to the last override group and rename the nodes as below in the rivet hierarchy.

- Select the cluster, then press **Ctrl+g** to group it.

- **Rename** this new group *upperLipCluster*.

- Select the *upperLipCluster* and the *rivet1* node, then press **Ctrl+g** to group them together.

- **Rename** this top node *upperLipClusterSetup*.

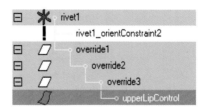

The rivet hierarchy

7 Connections

- **Connect** the sphere's **translate**, **rotate** and **scale** attributes to the cluster's **translate**, **rotate** and **scale** attributes.

- **Hide** the cluster's group.

8 Test the setup

The lips' controllers in action

> **Note:** Notice that the face controls will follow even when deforming the face, for instance, when using blend shapes.

9   Save your work

- Save your scene as *15-clusterOnMesh_02.ma*.

> **Note:**   *Watch the movie testAnimation.avi to see how the face control reacts.*

Conclusion

Now that you have experimented with creating controllers that follow a mesh perfectly, you can use this technique for other functions not limited to facial cluster animation.

In the next lesson, you will learn how to create a rolling lips setup.

Lesson 16 *The lips*

In this lesson, you will create a rolling lips setup with joints and driven keys. You will also rig a system to reproduce sticky lips. Implementing one or both of these techniques will significantly improve the quality of your character's facial animation and is well worth the time you spend applying it.

In this lesson you will learn the following:

- How to create a rolling lips setup;

- How to create a sticky lips setup;

- An overview of combining the rigs.

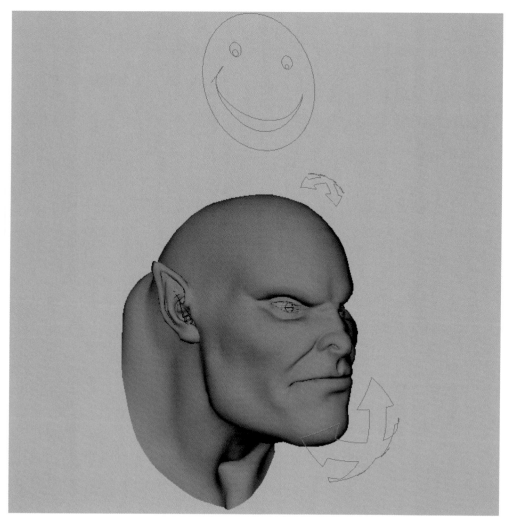

The combined facial rig

Rolling lips

The idea of a rolling lips setup is to rig a joint hierarchy that can be used with Set Driven Keys to create the effect of rolling the flesh, which would be hard to achieve otherwise.

The following explains the basics of creating a rolling lips setup.

1   Joint hierarchy

First, you must create a joint hierarchy that will be able to do the motion that you need.

▪ Open the scene *16-rollingLips_01.ma*.

The lips' joints are already created in that scene file.

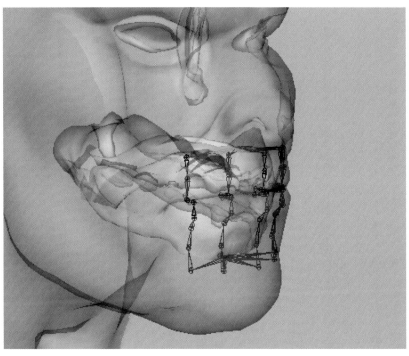

The lips' joint hierarchy

2   Binding the lips

You must now spend some time painting a small amount of weight per joint to allow for good deformation.

3   Set Driven Keys

Now that you have the lips properly skinned, you must create a controller object, such as a locator, with a custom attribute that will be used to drive the joints' rotations.

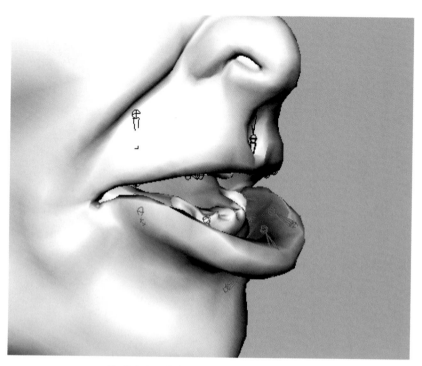

The lip being rolled outward by the driven keys

In order to achieve that specific movement, you need to use rotations or else it might not look as real as you would like it to. You could model multiple in-between blend shapes, but then you are stuck with more work than necessary since it is usually faster to weight some joints into the lips to get the rolling effect.

4   Corrective shape

It is highly recommended that once the setup smoothly rolls the lips to your desired point that you do a corrective blend shape to get the exact rolled open lip appearance that will keep the character looking real. You can then hook that blend shape with the driving attribute to have the corrective shape enabled when you rotate the lips outward.

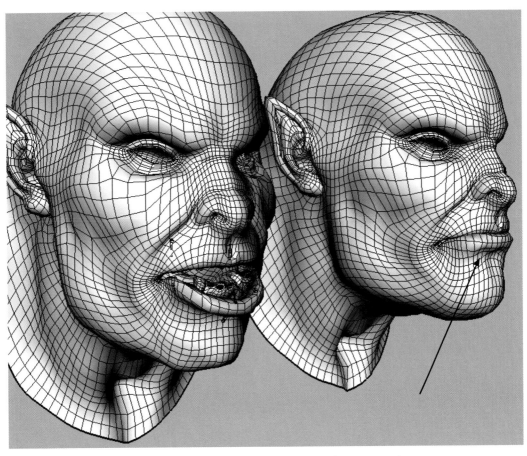

The corrective blend shape used to puff the lip as it rotates outward

Movie: *You can open the scene file 16-rollingLips_02.ma to see the final effect. You can also watch the movie rollingLips.avi to see the animated version of the setup.*

Sticky lips

The sticky lips setup presented here is the final and most involved section of the geometric rigging portion of this project. The sticky lips are meant to be the final touch on the facial rig, and due to the technique used, should also be applied at the very end of the deformation chain. Sticky lips should always be the last deformer so that they apply their effect on the final position of the lips in order to stay stuck together properly.

Note that sticky lips are meant to be controlled by the animator. There is a common misconception that they should be dynamic or even automated. Unfortunately, it is not a very productive way to get good facial animation. Animators know exactly how and when they want the lips to be sticky, and therefore the means to make them sticky is what you will be rigging. A completely user controlled attribute will be the result that will allow the animator to stick and separate the inner regions of the lips together in a non-linear manner at any time during the animation process.

The rig will take special care to get an appropriate centerline for the lips so that the fact that they have world space deformation precedence over the subtle inner skin lining the inside edge portion of the lips does not distract from the desired shape of the lips prior to the application of stickiness.

Note: *This exercise can be quite heavy and can slow down your computer's refresh rate.*

1   Scene file

- Open the scene file *16-stickyLips_01.ma*.

This scene contains the latest skinned beast's head, with blend shapes and face controls. The important thing to have in your working file is a proper jaw weighting.

2   Rivets

You will now use the *rivet.mel* script seen in the last lesson to determine the midpoint between the two lips.

- **Rotate** the jaw joint in order to have the mouth partially opened.

- Select a horizontal polygonal edge on the upper lip's outline, then select a correspondent edge on the lower lip, and then **execute** `rivet` in the Command Line.

Note: *Make sure you choose the outer edge of the lip, which will be the edge line loop of the lip's outline. Be sure not to select any edge that is directly connected to any vertices that you plan to be sticky. It is okay if the edge is in the same face as a vertex you plan on making sticky, as long as the edge you are picking is not directly affected by one of the sticky lip vertices when the vertex is moved.*

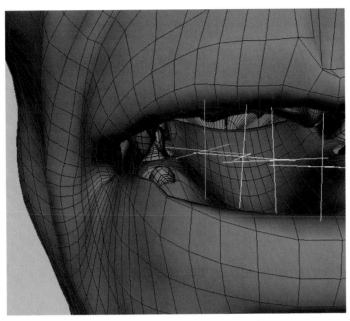

Edges to select to use with the rivet.mel script

Tip: It doesn't matter if the top and bottom edge don't perfectly match. The goal is to attempt to form the mouth's centerline at any point during any deformation, including O shapes and irregular bent or curled lip lines.

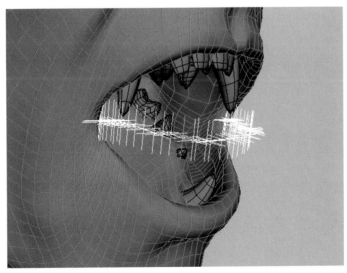

The mouth's centerline

3 Tweak the locators

You can delete the aim constraints that are on the rivets since they are not required, and orient constrain each locator to the upper and lower jaw joints. You can use a really simple MEL loop to automate this. Doing so, a task which could possibly take an hour is reduced to a few seconds.

- Select all the locators.

- **Type** the following script in the Script Editor and **execute** it.

> **Tip:** The following script can be found in the support files with explanations.

> **Note:** Make sure to type the first line of the script to reflect the proper upper and lower joint names.

```
string $constraint_objs[] = {"jaw_lower", "jaw_upper"};

string $selected_rivets[] = `ls -sl`;

for($each in $selected_rivets)

{

    delete `listRelatives -type aimConstraint $each`;

    select -r $constraint_objs;

    select -add $each;

    orientConstraint -offset 0 0 0 -weight 1 ;

    scale -r 0.2 0.2 0.2 $each;

}
```

4 Sticky lips head

- **Duplicate** an un-deformed head.

- **Rename** this new head to *stickyLipsHead*.

- Select the vertices of the model that you want to be sticky and select **Create** → **Sets** → **Set** to make a selection set out of them.

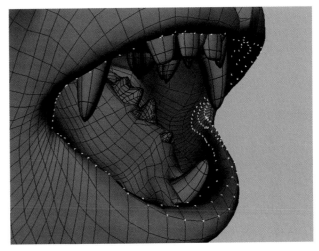

- **Rename** the new selection set to *stickyLipsVerts*.

You will be using this selection set later on.

The lips' vertices to be used for the sticky lips setup

> **Tip:** You can use a blend shape from the model with the jaw in it onto the new base shape model to temporarily open the mouth while selecting the vertices. Make sure to delete the blend shape node and completely close the mouth on the jaw model prior to Step 7.

5 Isolate the mouth faces

In this step you will set the view options to isolate the faces on which you want to work. Doing so will make it easier to work on the lips.

- With the lips' vertices still selected, select **Edit Polygons** → **Selection** → **Convert Selection To Face**.

> **Tip:** You can also convert the selection to faces by pressing *Ctrl+F11*.

- With the faces selected, turn **On** the **Show** → **Isolate Select** → **View Selected** and the **Show** → **Isolate Select** → **Auto Load New Objects**.

With the lip faces isolated, it is much easier to work on this single set of vertices in the mouth, without actually deleting faces or changing the vertex order of the model.

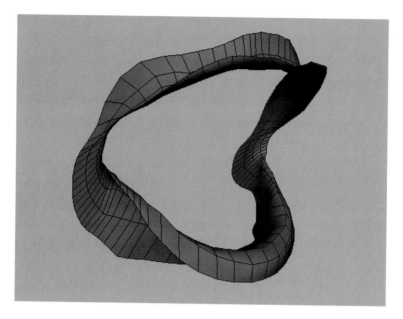

The isolated mouth faces

- When you are finished working on the lip faces, you can simply deactivate this viewing mode.

6 Clusters

- **Create** a **cluster** on each row of vertices all around the mouth of the model.

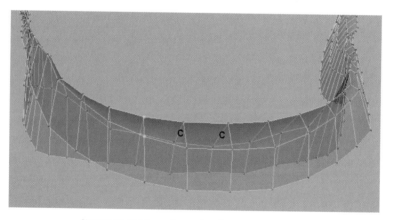

Clusters created for each row of vertices around the mouth

Note: You should only select the same vertices you defined in the previous step as the sticky lips vertices and not the outer rim vertices since those are used by the rivet locators. Otherwise, an evaluation cycle may occur.

7   Parenting the clusters

- With the head back to its default shape, parent each cluster to its closest rivet locator transform.

The reason for parenting the clusters is so that they will now move around with the center lip line of the model. This means that you will now have a deforming portion of the lips that stays centered on them no matter what the lip shape may be.

Note: *It doesn't matter if the clusters and the locators don't match perfectly. Try to parent the clusters to the closest locator.*

You should get the following warning when you parent the clusters, and it can be safely disregarded:

```
// Warning: clusters were grouped to preserve position //
```

It basically tells you that a group is now between the cluster and its parent in order to keep its exact same transformation matrix in space.

8   Control attribute

- Create a **locator**.

- **Add** a custom attribute and name it *stickyLips* with a **float** type.

This will eventually be the final control attribute of the setup.

- **Rename** the locator to *stickyLipsControl*.

9   Output head

- **Duplicate** another un-deformed head and **rename** it *outputHead*.

- Select the original skinned head, then **Shift-select** the *outputHead*.

- **Create** a blend shape deformer and set the new blend shape's attribute to **1**.

Note: *The reason for applying the joint deformed model as a blend shape onto a new base shape model is solely to avoid a dependency graph cycle and cycle check warnings for the purpose of this example.*

10 Per-vertex blend shapes

You will now do something a little unconventional. You will create a single blend shape for each vertex in the selection set you made earlier from the *stickyLipsHead* on the *outputHead*.

Doing this may seem overly complicated at first glance, but it is actually very simple when you automate the process with a few lines of MEL scripting.

- Select the members of the *stickyLipsVerts* set.

- **Type** and **execute** the following script in the Script Editor.

> **Tip:**   *The following script can be found in the support files with explanations.*

> **Note:**   *Make sure the first three lines reflect the proper names in your scene.*

```
string $sourceModel = "stickyLipsHead";

string $targetModel = "outputHead";

string $controller = "stickyLipsControl";


string $selected[] = `ls -sl -fl`;

$selected = sort($selected);

for($vert in $selected)

{

    string $targetVert = `substitute $sourceModel $vert $targetModel`;

    string $attrName = `substitute "^.*\\[" $vert ""`;

    $attrName = "SL_"+`substitute "\\]$" $attrName ""` ;

    addAttr -ln $attrName -at double -min 0 -max 1 -dv 0 $controller;

    setAttr -e -keyable true ($controller+"."+$attrName);

    string $blendShapeNode[];

    select -r $vert $targetVert;

    $blendShapeNode = `blendShape -tc 0 -o world -name ($attrName +"_BS")`;

    connectAttr ($controller+"."+$attrName) ($blendShapeNode[0]+".w[0]");

}
```

Creating the blend shapes this way gives you exactly the type of driven per vertex shape control that you will need to shape the sticky lips as you want when the sticky lip custom attribute driver changes. The sticky lips setup will thus work at all times, in all cases, since you are inserting the sticky lips at the end of the deformation chain on the points in world space. It doesn't matter what random deformer may be operating on the face as an input (joints, clusters, blend shapes, sculpts, etc), the sticky lip controller will always stick them together properly, which is a main goal of properly rigged and controllable sticky lips.

11 Driven keys

- Open the Set Driven Key window.

- Load the *stickyLips* attribute created earlier as the driving attribute.

- Load all of the per-vertex **SL_###** attributes that the script automatically put on the control locator as the driven.

- Set the *stickyLips* attribute to **10**, then set all of the **SL_###** attributes to **1**.

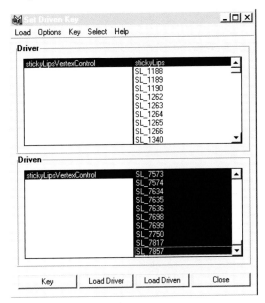

The loaded Set Driven Key window

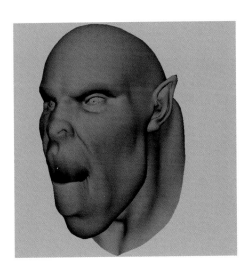

The fully sticking lips

- Click on the **Key** button.

- Set the *stickyLips* to **0**, then set the **SL_###** attributes to **0**.

- Click on the **Key** button.

12 Keyframing the shape of the sticky lips

Now you will begin to actually shape the sticky lips as they start to peel apart as the mouth opens. They should peel apart in an O shape, starting at the center and gradually un-sticking as they follow through to the edges at the mouth corners.

Using Set Driven Keys is perfect because they will result in smooth animation curves. You will thus be able to model the proper look of the sticky lips on a per-vertex level as each one falls in and out of stickiness.

- Set the *stickyLips* attribute to **3**.

- **Tweak** the attributes that control each vertex on the control locator, which will in turn shape the vertices on the mouth.

*At a value of **3**, you should have most of the center vertices not sticky and most of the vertices near the corner of the lips stuck together.*

Note: *The number in the attribute's name directly corresponds to the mesh's vertex number.*

- When you are done, click the **Key** button in the Set Driven Key window.

- **Repeat** so that you get the following main poses:

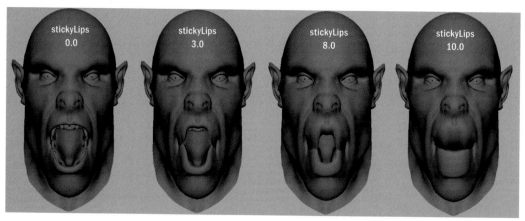

The main poses defined with Set Driven Keys

- **Add** as many in-between Set Driven Keys as you require.

- Lastly, **tweak** the actual Set Driven Keys' animation curves and set their tangent values in the Graph Editor to get the proper animation as you change the *stickyLips* attribute slider.

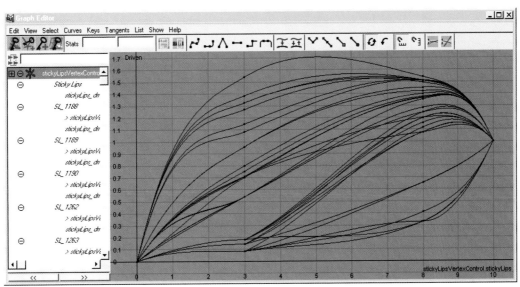

The animation curves in the Graph Editor

12 Save your work

- The final scene file is *16-stickyLips_02.ma*.

This scene contains two hidden heads, one with a rigged jaw and another one with the sticky lips setup. Those two heads are then piped in the final head as blend shapes and animated.

Movie: *Watch the movie stickyLips.avi from the support files for a simple example of what the sticky lips should look like when animated.*

Creating the final facial setup

In the examples of this project, you have created all the different setups into separate files. You shall now combine them into a single character setup file.

All that needs to be done is importing each one of the separate rig files into the rig with the jaw joint in it. Most likely this file will already have the cluster on meshes rigged into it as well as the sticky lips. So, you will need to import the blend shape models, the blinks, the fleshy eyes, the rolling lips, and any other facial rigging component that you may have completed in a separate file.

Next, select all of the models that are the outputs of the deformations of each one of the separate rigging components, and do a blend shape onto the facial model that has the *skinCluster* node that deforms the jaw to open the mouth. Be sure to do a front of chain blend shape. Next, create and connect any controller nodes, and hook up your attributes so they are easily exposed to the user.

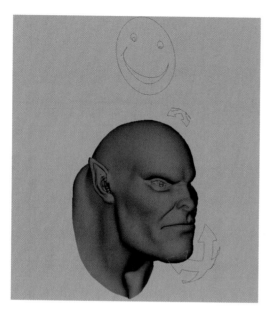

The combined facial rig

There are two basic rigging concepts that you should be using when creating the final setup file:

1 Iconic representation for character controls

No one should need to search for a control in your rig; they should be obvious and stick out to the user.

2 Prevent inappropriate manipulations

You should always consolidate, lock and hide non-keyable attributes so that items not meant to be touched remain hidden.

Note: Open the file named *16-facialRigCombined.ma* to see a completed version of the facial rig.

There are a few special connections that you could end up making when connecting the rigs together. For instance, the eyes had to be orient constrained to the fleshy eye joints. You will also need to set a driven key on the **envelope** attribute of the fleshy eyes' blend shape so that when the blink attribute is equal to **1**, the envelope value is equal to **0**, and when the blink is **0**, the envelope value is **1**.

Note: *The envelope attribute of the blend shape basically turns the entire blend shape off, so that as the eye blinks it doesn't get double transforms applied to it from both the blink and the fleshy eye setup.*

This technique can be used in many places with utility nodes or expressions to achieve the proper behavior in parts of the rig.

The rest of the attribute connections are pretty straightforward and don't require a detailed explanation. They can probably be achieved either with a direct connection or a Set Driven Key if necessary.

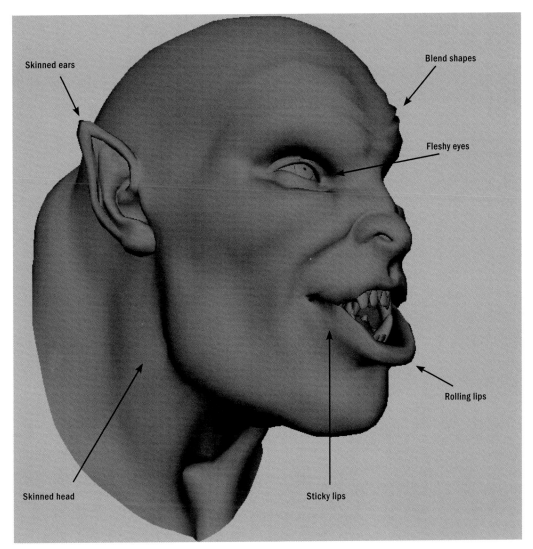

Skinned ears

Blend shapes

Fleshy eyes

Rolling lips

Skinned head

Sticky lips

All the different setups together

Conclusion

In this lesson, you learned techniques to rig the lips of a character. You first implemented rolling lips using joints and driven keys, and then you went through the task of creating an example of a sticky lips setup.

The techniques shown here are not the only ways of creating these sorts of effects. You should consider exploring other setup options in order to create your own custom facial rigs that will suit your needs.

In the next lesson, you will learn a driven displacement technique.

Lesson 17 *Driven displacement*

This lesson will teach you how to attain a high level of realism by tying your facial deformation rig with (and actually driving large parts of) the shading network. This is a fairly new technique that deserves considerable attention due to the complex reality it is attempting to duplicate. In real life, our skin's inherent shading parameters change their appearance as skin deforms around the bone, which causes the stretching and wrinkling over blood filled vessels and striated muscle tissue.

In this lesson you will learn the following:

- The definition of driven displacement;

- How to set-up driven displacement;

- How to build a shading network.

Driven displacement theory

Nowadays, in order to create believable hyper-real 3D characters, the effect of skin deformations should be synthesized as much as possible to achieve the desired look. High-end 3D characters must make use of driven displacement maps in order to recreate the phenomenon of deforming skin properties when animated.

It is possible to realize this powerful level of behavior with utility nodes, and then output a multi-pass render to an advanced photoreal film quality raytraced rendering engine, such as mental ray.

Facial expressions mixed with driven displacement maps

> **Note:** Open the scene file 17-drivenDisplacement.ma to see how the scene and its shading network was built and animated. This scene file references the three displacement maps found in the source image directory.

In the above image, the heightened level of realism made possible with custom displacement maps for each blend shape can easily be seen. These fine and detailed forms were sculpted like clay from the original models using painted displacement maps.

The idea is that the model is never meant to go to high resolution levels in its base mesh that could reach the level of detail needed for fine skin wrinkles (as seen in the examples above). The pock marks in the face, skin pores and wrinkled age lines that radiate downwards are beautiful examples of the types of additional elements that will guarantee the appearance of added realism to your rigged model when it renders.

The problem is that these kinds of details change considerably as the face shifts into different expressions. When you are attempting to make something look as real as possible as it is being animated, the different elements begin to fight each other. To counter that, you will see here that as each shape is animated, the same model can have an associated displacement map that will be blended in using a simple shading network. This shading network will basically emulate the blend shape algorithm that was covered in Lesson 12.

The UVs of the model are obviously very important in this entire lesson, and they need to be evenly laid out on the geometry so that the texture can be easily painted on. Even if your pipeline is using advanced third party projection paint texture software, you should still be sure that the model has nice UVs. The resulting effect quality will always look better if the UVs start out perfectly. The maps can only be as good as the 2D UV texture space that they have been painted into.

Here is what the displacement maps for one of the blend shapes look like, along with a UV snapshot of the same area. Take especial note that even this far way down the pipeline, a properly modeled edge flow that can be cleanly painted with appropriate maps for clean displacement tessellation at render time is of significant importance.

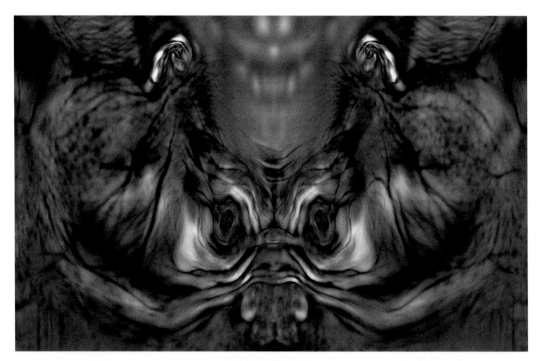

A displacement map

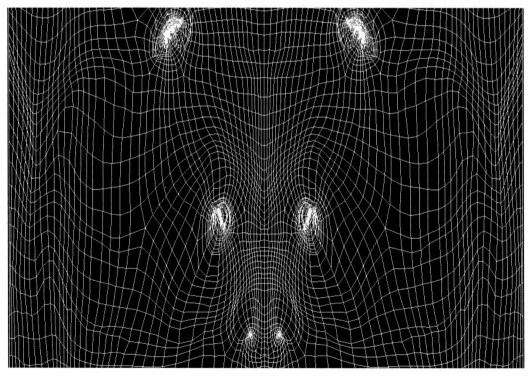

The head's UV mapping

Shading network

Now that you understand the necessity of having good UVs and a skin shader that reacts appropriately and can give the appearance of fine skin wrinkles when it deforms, you are faced with the challenge of rigging it up altogether. Luckily, the process is made extremely easy using built-in shading nodes. Similar to how deformers work automatically on every vertex in a 3D model to deform it, a shading node works on every sample in an image to process it much like a compositing operation during render time.

Basically, in order to make this whole process work as it should, your shading algorithm should echo exactly your deformation algorithm.

With this knowledge, you can go ahead and create a shading network that emulates the behavior of blend shapes. Then, use the multiplier that controls the blend shape attribute for a particular modeled shape to drive the multiplier that controls the calculated difference of a displacement map painted especially for that same modeled shape.

The simplicity of the blend shape algorithm can be built directly into the shading tree, as long as the original map is always started from the base map when modifying the new maps that get created. This is a perfectly reasonable requirement, since blend shapes already work that way. So, then all you have to do is subtract the original map from the newly painted map, making sure you subtract them in the right order so you are not getting incorrect negative values. You now have a difference vector, just like a blend shape has. Then you take the output of that subtract node and multiply it by the actual blend shape value. Next, all you need to do is take this output and add it in with all the other difference outputs from any of the other blend shapes, as well as the base shape. The outputs of this single add node should then be connected to the displacement and bump map's input channels.

The network explained above is delineated in the following Hypershade network. It uses a simple example with only two blend shapes for the sake of clarity. You can have an unlimited number of inputs coming in to that final add node that plugs into the displacement shader, and they will all work exactly as they should.

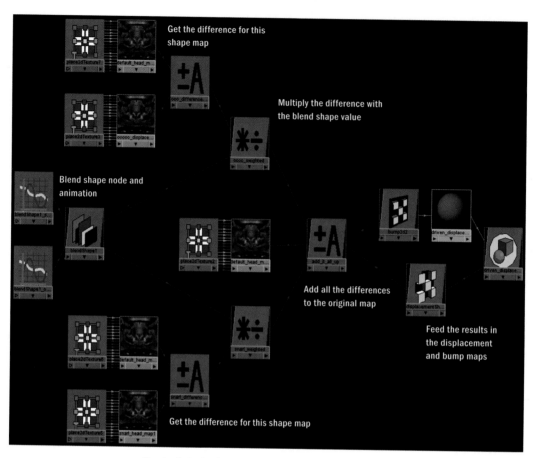

The shading network used to extract proper displacement values

Movie: *Watch the movie drivenDisplacement.mov from the support files to see an animated example of this technique.*

The rendered final effect

The rendered movie from the support file is only a test with low quality render settings. If certain approximation settings in mental ray's displacement subdivisions and raytracing settings in the Render Settings were made higher, there would be even richer shaded detail in the geometry.

Conclusion

In this lesson, you learned about animating facial textures with the facial setup in order to have a rich hyper-real skin deformation effect. You also learned about building a shading network that emulates the blend shape algorithm as a way to blend texture maps together.

You should seriously consider using such a technique for any hyper-real characters, but not limiting yourself to such implementation. Driven displacement can be used in several scenarios and adds a special touch that makes a character hyper-real.

In the next lesson, you will review some other tricks and techniques for achieving successful hyper-real characters.

Lesson 18 *Expanded topics*

This lesson covers additional tricks and techniques to potentially raise the level of realism of your rendered images. You will first learn about creating a realistic skin look using render passes and compositing. You will then learn about faking an iris refraction using a simple trick that will allow you to see the effect of the refraction without having to render your scene.

In this lesson you will learn the following:

- Concepts of a realistic skin shader;

- How to fake an iris refraction.

Hyper-real skin

Realistic skin shader

The goal of a good skin shader is to achieve what is called *sub-surface scattering*. Sub-surface scattering is the technical term for the effect of light reaching the skin, penetrating it, getting scattered in the flesh and then emerging with a fleshy color that may vary from place to place on the body, especially in the facial area. Although there is no direct mathematical calculation for explicitly calculating a sub-surface algorithm, you will now learn about building your own skin shader network.

In order to achieve a decent skin shader, it is recommended to use a renderer such as mental ray, which offers ambient occlusion, final gathering and global illumination. Combining those render passes together will ultimately achieve a decent looking fake sub-surface scattering.

The explanations given here will cover the idea behind the technique and not the technique itself. This will leave you with your own impression of a good skin shader, thus letting you devise the specific technique required by your production.

The following image was extremely simple to render and took very little time or effort using the mental ray renderer.

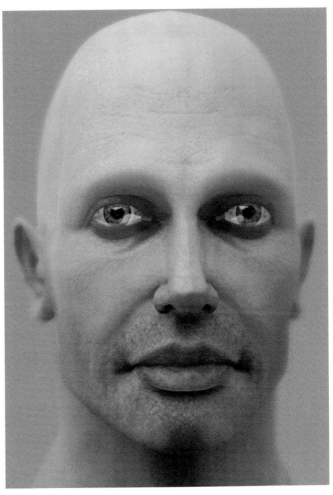

Hyper-real skin shader using the mental ray renderer

Tip: The ambient occlusion was rendered using a custom shading node for the mental ray renderer. In order to achieve the exact same effect as what is shown here, you might have to consider getting some custom tools that will do what you require.

Note: All the images shown in this example can be found in the images directory from the support files.

The first step for creating good looking skin is to construct good textures to be used to shade your model. The following textures have almost no specular highlight in them and only a trace of shadows. Careful consideration was taken to get a good color map for the skin with some nice natural hues in it.

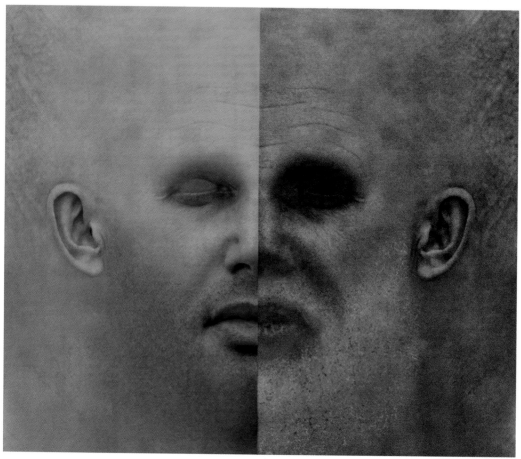

The color and bump texture maps

The diffuse render pass of the model is then rendered using mental ray with several area lights that have really high diffuse values on all the objects' shaders. This produced the following image:

The diffuse render pass

Then, a light blue-green hue was used in the specular color channel. The specular channel was also occluded in compositing using the ambient occlusion and final gathering pass. The key to this look really happens when you layer the diffuse color pass (which purposefully is rendered without any bump map), with the specular pass (which is rendered with high bump values as well as a nice looking sheen from image based specular reflections). The final gathering and ambient occlusion pass is layered in such a way that it works more like specular occlusion than shadow.

The following shows the compositing layers.

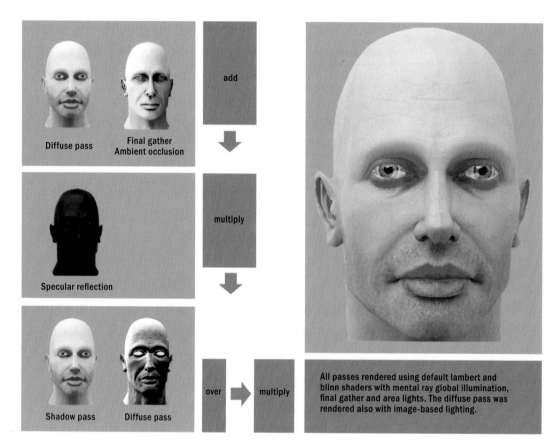

Diffuse pass

Final gather
Ambient occlusion

add

Specular reflection

multiply

Shadow pass

Diffuse pass

over

multiply

All passes rendered using default lambert and blinn shaders with mental ray global illumination, final gather and area lights. The diffuse pass was rendered also with image-based lighting.

The compositing of the render passes to achieve the final image

Note: *The final compositing passes can be examined in the Adobe® Photoshop® file photoshop_comp.psd from the images directory in the support files.*

Fake iris refraction

The difficulty of realistic eye refraction done using real bent rays and raytracing in a shading model is not its ability to look real; instead, the problem is that it is near impossible to be previewed by the animator, who is the one setting the exact position of where the eyes will be looking.

The possibility exists to realistically fake the eye refraction directly in the scene, using simple deformers and some vector product nodes. This is possible since the eye is basically a spherical surface, and it is fairly easy to convincingly fake refraction through the tip of a round object such as the eye. Since the eyeball geometry is two separate surfaces, it works by simply using driven blend shapes and sculpt deformers, which are driven from the dot product and angle between the eye to camera vector and some simple weighted vectors that fall in-between. The mirror across the eye vector is also useful for deforming the geometry on the other side of the eye where it may have some intersection problems with the outer eye surface.

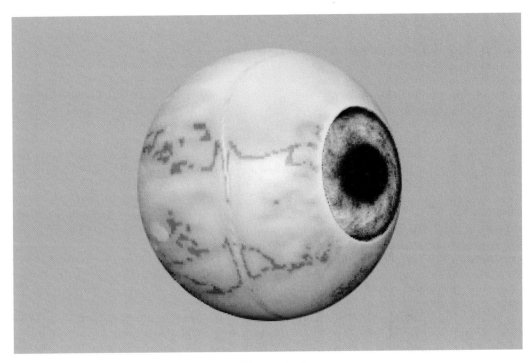

The fake eye refraction

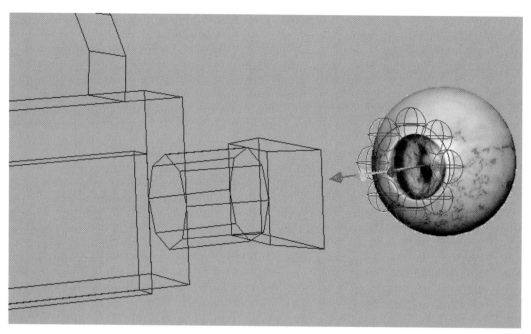

The fake eye refraction setup

> **Movie:** Watch the movies fakeEyeRefraction.avi and fakeEyeRefractionAltView.avi to understand how this effect is achieved.

The idea behind doing this was based on tricks used for faking refraction on a character with very large eyes, and for which the resulting position of the iris might have affected the direction of an animation. The trick shown here is done directly in the model and is much simpler and less realistically accurate. If this is done using enough surface resolution it can look reasonably believable, and the key is that the animator can immediately see it in the viewport without any additional rendering or problems when it comes to posing the eyes. Hence, discrepancies between where the black part of the pupil will be once it is passed through a refraction shader can be avoided.

Conclusion

In this lesson, you have seen that it is possible to reach the expected result by not following the all-in-one rendering solution. There are shortcuts. You can easily fake your way into building believable effects by creatively mining your own experiences and resources. This is something that becomes more comfortable over time.

In truth, there are no limits to how setups can be made, especially if the design of the character involved has different challenges than the near-human creature presented here.

The fact is, this book covers straightforward anatomically based 3D artistic theory and mid-level software usage technique. Nothing throughout the book should be un-accessible to the familiar Maya user. The techniques explained here work successfully. They are based on many years of combined experience and their success has been proven in major feature films across various digital production facilities. In a line, this book's goal has been to use generic, extendable and technically conceptual ways to approach facial setup and deformation rigging to achieve relatively modest, but usually believable results.

"Imagination is more important than knowledge."

-Albert Einstein

Index

Notes

Maya™ 7

changing the face of 3D

Alias®

New Old School

The natural way to draw,
the modern way to work.

Alias® SketchBook™ Pro, the high quality paint and drawing tool for use with tablet PC's and digitized tablets, has a fast, simple and natural interface that has the tactile feel of drawing with a pencil and paper and all the benefits of a digital format.

The artist friendly, gesture-based user interface of SketchBook Pro is easy enough for the casual user to master, yet has all the features that experts demand. But don't take our word for it. Download a full-featured trial version of SketchBook Pro 2 for Mac® or Windows® at **www.alias.com/sketchbookpro** and try it for yourself.

Alias
SketchBook Pro 2

Alias® | www.alias.com

GET MORE OUT OF MAYA®

with the Maya Silver Membership program!

As award-winning software, Maya® is the most comprehensive 3D and 2D graphics and animation solution on the market. And whether you're using Maya Personal Learning edition to learn more about computer graphics and animation, or you have a full Maya license that you're using to produce professional content, the Maya Silver Membership program helps you take your Maya skill to the next level.

What is Maya Silver Membership?

Your Maya Silver Membership program gives you quick, online access to a wide range of Maya learning resources. These educational tools – in-depth tutorials; real-life, project-based learning materials; the Maya Mentor learning environment plug-in; Weblogs from experienced Maya users – are available for a fixed monthly, or cost-saving annual, subscription fee.

Silver Membership also keeps you abreast of the latest computer graphics industry developments and puts you in touch with other Maya users and industry experts. Plus, you get 30 days of personal help to orient you around the site.

Key Benefits

- **Unbeatable Value**
- **Faster Learning**
- **Competitive Advantage**
- **Industry Contacts**

© Grey Advertising 2005

Silver Membership Features

Downloadable Learning Tools
Silver members now have access to selected Learning Tools, at no charge.

Project-based Learning Materials
A wide range of up-to-date, online learning materials takes you through sample projects. Step-by-step new projects are published each month!

Tutorials Database
This extensive, sort-able database provides access to over 100 Maya tutorials created by Alias Product Specialists and industry experts.

Concierge Program
Silver membership entitles you to 30 days of personal, one-on-one access to a site attendant who will help you learn how to best use the online resources of the Silver Membership program.

Duncan's Corner
You can now learn from Alias' own Principal Scientist – Duncan Brinsmead. This Silver-exclusive Weblog will feature workflow tips as well as demo files and example files from the man behind such important Maya innovations as Maya Paint Effects™ and Maya Fluid Effects™.

Alias® Weblogs
Interact with industry leaders or Product Specialist to discuss how they created a particular work using Maya.

Industry Knowledge Articles
These articles include interviews and stories on industry-related topics.

Textures & Shaders Database
Silver members will have access to a new collection of extremely high-resolution (2048 x 2048), tile-able textures and shaders that are ready for use in production or on any Maya project.

Discussion Forums
Join in a Silver Membership discussion forum, hosted by an experienced 3D artist or instructor, and get answers on questions related to the learning materials.

Personal gallery page
Annual subscribers are also entitled to post a personal gallery page on the alias.com site that lets them share personal information and Maya images they've created with other members of the Maya community.

Bonus Offers
As a Silver member you receive bonus magazine subscriptions with your membership. Plus all members who take out an annual membership receive, in addition to their magazine subscription, a bonus Maya Learning Tool.

For pricing and other information regarding the Maya Silver Membership program: **www.alias.com/silver**

Hyper-Realistic Production Series I & II

From modeling to rendering, the Hyper-Real series brings to life a frighteningly realistic, nightmare-inducing beast. Learn how the experts get the results they want, through titles authored by Erick Miller, Sony Pictures Imageworks, Paul Thuriot, EA, Jeff Unay, Weta, Rudy Grossman, Weta, Andy Jones, Sony Pictures Imageworks and more…

ALIAS INDUSTRY SOLUTIONS GUIDE

Maya TECHNIQUES

SuperToon Series

Maya Techniques™ | SuperToon DVD Series If squishy faces, rolling tongues, squashing bellies and stretchy limbs are your challenge, then the *Maya Techniques | SuperToon DVD Series* is for you. Master the cartoon landscape and defy the laws of the physical world with this three part series written by industry professionals

 www.alias.com/learningtools

Alias | LearningTools

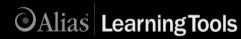